# The
# Peaceful
# Home

Country Living

# The Peaceful Home

Alice Westgate
Photography by Paul Ryan

Hearst Books

New York

All first editions are printed on acid-free paper.

The acknowledgments that appear on page 192 are hereby made a part of this copyright page.
The publisher wishes to thank the owners, designers, and friends who opened their doors for
photography. A special thank you to Juliana Balint for her help and organization.

Library of Congress Cataloging-in-Publication Data
Country living the peaceful home / the editors of Country living magazine. -- 1st ed.
        p.    cm.
    Includes index.
    ISBN 0-688-15618-5
1.  Decoration and ornament,  Rustic--United States.
2.  Interior decoration--United States.
I. Country living (New York, N.Y.)
NK2002.C624  1998
747--dc21                                                    97-21898
                                                                 CIP


Printed and bound in Italy by LEGO S.p.A.

*Country Living* Staff
Rachel Newman, Editor-in-Chief
Nancy Mernit Soriano, Executive Editor
Julio Vega, Art Director
Mary R. Roby, Managing Editor
Marjorie E. Gage, Features and Arts & Antiques Editor
Robin Long Mayer, Senior Editor/Decorating and Design
John Mack Carter, President, Hearst Magazine Enterprises


Produced by
Marshall Editions, 170 Piccadilly, London W1V 9DD
**Project editor**   Jane Chapman
**Art editor**   Patrick Carpenter
**DTP editor**   Lesley Gilbert
**Managing editor**   Lindsay McTeague
**Editorial director**   Sophie Collins
**Art director**   Sean Keogh
**Production**   Nikki Ingram


FIRST EDITION

10  9  8  7  6  5  4  3  2  1

# Contents

# Introduction

Your home should be a refuge from the stresses of the outside world. It should be a place that nurtures you, calms you, pleases you, and indulges you – a haven of constancy and calm when all around you is unpredictable and demanding. Providing you with a sense of belonging, your home is a place where you can establish roots, grow, and flourish. While bricks and mortar in themselves can't make you happy, a well-designed home that is filled with things you love is a solid foundation on which to build a rich and rewarding life.

You don't have to spend lots of money, follow a particular trend, adhere to any prescribed principles, or strive for anyone else's idea of

● A peaceful home is a place where you feel happy and at ease because you have struck a comfortable balance between what you need, what you love, and what is practical.

perfection. Creating a peaceful home is all about self-expression – trusting your instincts and developing your own style, whether you live in a cottage or a castle. All you need do is be yourself and make choices from the heart. Spontaneity and idiosyncrasy are the secrets of success.

The first step is to imagine what your perfect house would be like – its style, size, location, and atmosphere. The second is to enhance the quality of the experience by satisfying the senses, incorporating wonderful sights, sounds, scents, tastes, and textures at every opportunity. The final step is to recognize the practicalities that will turn your ideas into reality.

The three parts of this book – "The Options," "The Senses," and "The Basics" – will guide you along the path toward creating a home that is more peaceful than you have ever dreamed.

● Mind, body, and spirit are at peace in a bedroom whose decorative scheme is a spontaneous expression of the owner's individual style.

# PART ONE

# The Options

To design and decorate a house successfully you need a vision – a picture in your mind's eye of the most blissful place imaginable.

Retreat here in a dreamy moment to think about what life would feel like and what your surroundings would look like, decorating and furnishing as you go. You are not subject to any real-life constraints, so you can have whatever you have always wanted. By adding things that make your home seem as relaxing as possible, and by getting rid of anything that causes stress, you can explore your ideals and build on them. Remember that it takes more than a good location and an attractive exterior to make you feel truly at home – the deepest sense of well-being often comes from the smallest details.

● A welcoming kitchen and a relaxing living space are central to many visions of a peaceful home.

Without a clear view of what sort of home really appeals to you, it is easy to be swayed by other people's ideas of perfection and to be influenced by the images that bombard you whenever you go shopping or turn on the television set. It's tempting to choose one of these looks and import it wholesale, but this is not an honest reflection of your needs and tastes. Instead, allow inspiration to come from a number of sources, choosing things that please you or have a special meaning – a picture in a magazine, the colors in a painting, a pebble found on a beach, a photograph of a favorite place. No matter how varied and unconventional the look, it will be unique to you, and that is what matters.

Next, notice all the things that help make your imaginary home a pleasurable place to be – delicious food, uplifting music, enticingly scented flowers, plenty of books, comfortable chairs. Make a conscious decision to integrate these things into your new life – if you don't, it's easy to compromise more and more in the face of daily demands until eventually you exclude the things that do you a world of good.

When you find something that brings your vision to life – a paint color, a certain type of flooring, a particular piece of fabric – this should be placed at the heart of your peaceful home. If you can only reach your goal by changing something more fundamental, now may be the time to consider making some structural improvements or even moving to a new house. Whatever you do, you can't go wrong if you keep your vision in the forefront of your mind.

● Developing a strong sense of personal style is the key to decorating with flair. Introduce a few well-loved and unexpected elements to give your living space an original twist.

# what sort of home?

It's easy to describe the sort of home you want in terms of the number of bedrooms it has, its age, and its location, and to find many places that meet these criteria. But it is more difficult to specify a property's "feel," to describe how you want the space to work and to identify its sense of style. Yet these are the things that make you fall in love with a place and want to stay there for a lifetime.

To see how well your house compares to your vision of the perfect, peaceful home, write down everything that you like and dislike about it, then ask yourself the following questions. Do some of the rooms get used more than others? Can the ones that are not working well be put to better use? Is there room to accommodate guests? Is there enough space to work from home? Is there adequate storage space? Is there enough natural light? Has the lighting been planned properly? Is the equipment for simple chores such as laundry and cooking easily accessible? Is the house well soundproofed and acoustically healthy? Does it include a special corner devoted to relaxation? Does it tend to feel warm or cold? Do you have enough space outdoors? Above all, how comfortable – or how stressful – is it?

● Three very different interiors each display their own peaceful qualities. A bedroom with white walls, cool wood, and natural light is a beautifully simple approach (opposite). Old-fashioned formality creates a bedroom that will cocoon you in its warm colors and rich fabrics (left above). Traditional country style presents artifacts from the past in a more casual manner, giving a natural, wholesome, and lived-in feeling (left below).

15

Your responses to these questions will help identify any areas of tension and conflict, allowing you to resolve them and then move toward a healthier, more comfortable way of life. But remember that there is no formula for designing a peaceful home, because everyone's needs and expectations are so different.

How you feel about your surroundings is more important than conforming to one particular style. For example, there's no reason why a sophisticated urban apartment should be less conducive to relaxation and peace of mind than a picturesque house in the country. A quiet life of rural isolation does not appeal to everyone, yet for some it is the epitome of tranquility.

Neither are there any rules about minimally decorated rooms being automatically more restful than those that are full of pattern and possessions. An interior painted in neutral shades with few pieces of furniture might set one person on edge, while another would feel clear-headed and serene. A brimful farmhouse kitchen might be the perfect informal room to some, but an unbearable muddle to others. Old-fashioned style has devotees who like to feel in touch with the past, preferring traditional craftsmanship to a modern, pristine finish, while modernists are passionate about the immediacy of contemporary style and are quite happy with the high-tech or synthetic. What's more, you can mix any of these styles together – urban and rustic, natural and high-tech – or be a purist. The choice is yours.

● Styles do not have to be reproduced slavishly. In the living rooms of a city apartment (opposite) and a rustic log house (left), old and new co-exist together comfortably.

The age of your house may help you decide on the ideal style for its decoration – in fact, the proportions of its rooms might already give it a certain mood. But are spacious, light, and airy rooms more restful than smaller, more intimate ones? It all depends on your response to space – only you can judge if high ceilings seem imposing or elegant and if low ones feel cozy or claustrophobic.

Do you want a house that is full of color or one that uses subtle neutrals? It's tempting to shy away from using vivid shades in rooms that are set aside for relaxation, but a bright color may be the perfect choice. Intense sea blues, deep forest greens, or fresh yellows can form the backdrop to the most tranquil of rooms, where pastels would seem half-hearted. However, in some situations – perhaps in a bedroom or a study – being surrounded by gentle colors might promote rest or clarity of thought. Just choose whatever puts you in the right frame of mind: neutral, vibrant, pastel, or monochromatic.

All these factors, from the purely practical to the decadently decorative, help to make the mood of your house far more flexible than you may have thought possible. They all have a profound effect on your emotions, so choose wisely and any home can become a place where mind as well as body can find solace.

● Rooms with high ceilings aren't necessarily imposing. In this lofty living room, bookcases and a stone fireplace echo the scale of a room with more conventional proportions. This, along with plenty of wood, stone, and fabric, give the area a surprising sense of warmth and intimacy.

# finding a balance

If you are struggling to reconcile your love of uncluttered, minimalist interiors with the demands of a growing family, if you long to experience the country dream even though your work ties you to the city, or if you live in a modern house but have a passion for traditional interiors, how can you find a balance? To reduce the clutter in a family home, use your ingenuity to find extra storage solutions that will keep toys and games out of sight when they are not in use. Evenings can then become the time for the house to take on a more ordered – and, if you are very neat – even a minimal look. Try to decorate rooms in plain, light colors and keep them free from unnecessary ornaments and rarely used pieces of furniture. Set aside the largest bedroom for children rather than adults so they can have a generous amount of space as their playroom.

If you feel out of place in the city, compensate for the lack of outdoor greenery by planting a colorful flower-filled windowbox. Noise pollution can be reduced by improving your home's soundproofing, while the frenetic pace of life can be eased by filling the air with scent from relaxing essential oils. To mitigate the gray urban landscape, you could paint your walls in vibrant Mediterranean colors.

If you have a new house but long for more old-fashioned surroundings, filling your home with reproduction furniture and fixtures is not necessarily the best solution. Instead, bear in mind that a few old things can complement new ones, softening their lines and counteracting their perfection. An old sofa will become the focus of an otherwise plain modern living room; inherited china will look pretty against a simple white wall; antique bed linen will add character to a new loveseat; and a scrubbed pine table will echo another age even in a high-tech kitchen.

When you find this sort of balance, compromise is easy to live with. The secret is not to take any particular style too literally, but to go for a "taste" of the look you want. Something is always better than nothing.

● One or two well-placed pieces of furniture can be enough to conjure up a particular style or atmosphere. This whimsical daybed becomes the focal point of an otherwise sparsely furnished room.

# moving

You might consider moving in order to acquire the living space of your dreams – even though, paradoxically, the planning, negotiating, and upheaval can be extremely stressful. Try to see a move as a great opportunity to make a fresh start. In particular, moving allows you to make choices based on your present needs, which may well have changed since you last moved. It also encourages you to focus your hopes and aspirations, and is a great chance to restructure, reorder, and reorganize your life and your possessions for the better.

Moving also gives you the chance to gain more living space – both indoors and out. An extra bedroom, a separate dining room, a bigger kitchen, more storage space, a larger yard – these can all make a huge difference in your quality of life. You might also want to move to a new area that is quieter or more countrified, or somewhere that is closer to your friends or relatives or more convenient for work, schools, or shopping. If you are thinking of leaving city life behind and "getting away from it all," try not to underestimate the commitment this requires. If your work still ties you to a city, you may spend hours traveling every day and have little time to enjoy the benefits of your new country home. You might be better off moving instead to a place with a bigger backyard in which to enjoy the outdoor life.

When looking for a new property, try to visit at different times of the day to see how much sun the house and yard get, and how traffic and other external noises affect it. Imagine where your furniture will fit, how you will use the rooms, and whether the space will still suit you in the years to come. Look at the potential for converting the attic or basement, building an extension, or changing a room's use. Upstairs bedrooms often make sunny multipurpose rooms, small kitchens and dining rooms can be combined into one room, sunrooms or enclosed porches can be used as dining rooms, and a tiny bedroom can be turned into a quiet, book lined study.

Once you have moved in, take time to grow accustomed to the feel of the new house before you begin to decorate. When you are used to its character, its setting, its light, and its space, you can judge what colors, patterns, and textures are needed. Your new home is like a blank canvas on which you can paint whatever picture you choose.

● Take advantage of a move to improve the quality and size of your living space – a generously sized kitchen is a high priority for many people.

# staying put

Making a few changes – some radical, others subtle – can make it worthwhile staying in your present property and can even make you fall in love with it all over again.

If you feel you have outgrown your home, and that having more space would make life easier, think about building an extension, converting the attic, or adding a four-season porch. Creating a quiet room in which to work, an outdoor space for relaxing in, or an extra bedroom can impose order on a home that is straining at the

seams. Look at your living space with a fresh eye to see if any of these options would work for you.

Restructuring the space you already have could be another solution. If everyone tends to congregate in a tiny kitchen while an adjoining dining room is always empty, consider switching to a more open-plan design that gives you one large, versatile space in which to eat, socialize, and cook. A separate dining room and living room might also work much better as a single living area. A tiny storage room could be

transformed into a dressing room to free up bedroom space or into a connecting bathroom to provide a luxurious place to unwind at the end of the day.

If you feel that your house has lost some of its character, try to make the most of original features such as fireplaces, paneled doors, sash windows, decorative moldings, and picture rails – replacing them if necessary. These details will make a room come alive again. Natural materials such as wood and stone, seagrass and sisal, linen and cotton can also make your surroundings seem more appealing and peaceful, since they evoke memories of a simpler and healthier way of life.

So instead of chasing perfection from one house to the next, why not consider the possibilities in your present home?

● Make a virtue of a small space by turning it into a cozy cottage-style bedroom (right). Consider setting aside a generously proportioned first-floor area for an airy and uncluttered master bedroom (above).

# introducing change

Whether you are redesigning your old house or decorating a new one from scratch, every change you make should enhance its sense of calm and invite you to relax.

Adding one elegant piece of furniture will quickly establish a room's sense of style. Key pieces such as sofas, generous armchairs, and beds all show that comfort is your priority. Choose them carefully and each one will become a wonderful focal point.

Bring in new colors to give a sense of warmth, light, coziness, or serenity – even in neutral schemes, a vibrant throw, rug, length of fabric, or window treatment will enhance the room and catch the eye. Introduce different types of lighting, and colors will take on a new mood. Add pattern, and the space will appear to change. Mix in some texture, and things will take on another dimension.

Alter your impression of a room by rearranging the elements that are already there – change the position of the furniture, hang the pictures differently, vary the places you display your collections. Include a new floral arrangement or a plant, some decorative accessories, or a striking work of art to reflect your character and your style.

These changes, and all those set out in the pages that follow, are part of a subtle process that will transform your house from four plain walls to a richly rewarding and infinitely inspiring haven of peace and tranquility.

● Wooden floors, inviting armchairs, and a traditional fireplace combine to create a room with a focus and a house that has soul.

# PART TWO

# The Senses

Anyone who craves a peaceful home should become aware of the simple things that satisfy the senses and create a feeling of harmony. A home that does not look, feel, sound, taste, or smell appealing engenders tension and restlessness in the people who live there. They may not realize exactly why they are uncomfortable, but will discover that enhancing sensory pleasure in the home will lead to a greater sense of fulfillment.

It's difficult to be aware of the acute power of the senses because modern life – especially in towns and cities – can have a desensitizing effect. If you rarely smell the scent of a flower, look out to a distant horizon, or listen to the sound of the sea, you may forget that you ever loved these pleasures.

● Flowers, food, candles, color, pattern, and light

make a celebratory meal in a beautiful setting a

feast for the senses.

● Indulge in the things you love – an instinctive response to color is the basis for room plans with plenty of character.

Rediscovering what pleases and matters deeply to you is often the key to a happier and more contented sense of self, and your home should reflect this. You will feel more alert and alive when you are there.

It is possible to enhance your visual sense by drawing and painting. Both will help you to appreciate objects and will encourage you to explore color, form, perspective, pattern, light, and shadow. Do some colors inspire, calm, or agitate you? Do you find curves or straight lines more pleasing? Are you attracted to plain colors or busy patterns?

You can become more aware of the sounds around you by shutting your eyes and listening to the background noise you usually take for granted. Do you crave quiet, hating the intrusion of the wind, the buzz of traffic, or the chatter of people around you? Or do you hate silence, always preferring something, such as music, conversation, or the sounds of the outdoors, to "fill in" the space?

Your olfactory senses can be developed if you inhale a drop of essential oil and focus on exactly how it makes you feel. You may have an instant aversion to it, or know that you would be happy if it surrounded you. You may be aware that one fragrance helps you relax, while another revitalizes you. A particular aroma may evoke memories of the past, reminding you of certain people or places.

Taking time to enjoy a favorite food or savor the complex flavors of a glass of wine or a cup of coffee will challenge your taste buds. Can you describe the taste? What does it remind you of? How does it make you feel? Can you remember where you were when you first experienced it?

If you surround yourself with sensuous fabrics, you can enjoy their textures under your touch. Decide which are most comfortable to live with. Do you prefer soft carpet, warm wood, or cool stone under foot?

When you have identified the things you love, build your home around them. Decorating decisions based on these responses will seem effortless, and your house will become a sanctuary.

*"The linden and the plane, still decked with their summer finery, seemed clothed, the one in red velvet, the other in orange silk."*

GUY DE MAUPASSANT

# Sight

Look around you and be inspired by all that you see – color, light, texture, pattern, and shape. Nature offers a wealth of visual treats: bright poppies in a field; the soft light of a rosy sunset; the smoothness of water-washed pebbles; the geometry of a honeycomb; the gentle curves of a peach. Whether the sights you see are soothing or stimulating, familiar or alien, pleasing or unsettling, you react to them all.

Let the things you love to look at dictate the style and atmosphere of your home. Surround yourself with things that please your eye, lift your mood, or excite your senses: wonderful paint colors, intricate patterns, shapely furniture, sympathetic lighting, glorious fabrics, and complementary accessories. This is the perfect way to create a home that nourishes and nurtures you, a place that gives you a sense of well-being and the promise of peace of mind.

● Even a room that is blissfully simple must have color, texture, light, and pattern to satisfy the eye. Subtle touches, such as the yellow-patterned quilts, make this bedroom at once restrained and rich.

● Subdued pastels – such as pale blues and dusty pinks – are perfect for rooms intended for relaxation.

## Questions to ask before deciding on a room's color

- Is the room small or large?
- Does it have plenty of natural light?
- Does it face north, south, east, or west?
- Is it normally cold or warm?
- Do you use it for work or relaxation?
- Do you use it most during the day or at night?
- Does anything inside or nearby – a favorite piece of furniture, the view – inspire you or have a bearing on the room's character?
- Are you naturally drawn to a particular color?

# looking at color

The most profound way to alter a room is with color. Paint is the quickest and easiest option, giving your home a facelift and a change of atmosphere. Color has such a powerful effect on people that it is used therapeutically. Many public buildings are decorated with this in mind, and your home should be too. In addition to altering mood, effective use of color can compensate for negative factors such as lack of natural light or awkward proportions. Certain colors are also more appropriate to certain activities – a blue bedroom may be more restful than a red one, while a blue bathroom might seem too chilly. So before you choose a new color scheme, think about the room and the way you use it (see box).

## Understanding color

Color is an emotional subject, and a very personal one. Each part of the spectrum traditionally represents different moods: red is a byword for anger, people can be green with envy or suffer from the blues. It is tempting to shy away from using strong colors because of these powerful associations, but get the shade and the mix right and you'll have an interior that is alive and vibrant.

White light is composed of a spectrum of colors – red, orange, yellow, green, blue, indigo, and violet. Represented in a circle, this spectrum produces a color wheel, which helps you understand how colors work together. The reason a purple throw pillow blends well with a blue sofa is that these two colors are harmonious – they sit beside each other on the color wheel. A purple throw pillow on a yellow sofa, however, looks zingy because these two colors are complementary – they are opposite on the color wheel.

## Color and space

One of the basic decorating tenets is that intense, warm colors such as yellows, reds, and oranges advance, making objects seem closer, while cool shades of blue, green, gray, and purple recede. Apply this formula to open up a small attic room by painting the walls powder blue; or make an imposing hallway more inviting with a rich yellow on the walls. You can also pick out an interesting detail or disguise an unsightly feature by following this principle. The same optical illusions can be called into play for ceilings.

## Color and light

A room that gets little sunlight, or one that loses the best light after early morning, may need to be "warmed" with colors such as yellow, apricot, or terra cotta. Conversely, a room on the sunny side of the house may benefit from cooler colors such as sky blue and mint green. Add a touch of yellow pigment to blue and it won't be as chilly; add a touch of blue to red and you'll have a cooler cerise.

Another consideration is the time of day at which the room is used most. Early morning sun has a warm glow that can be intensified or played down by your decorating scheme. The light at noon is fairly neutral and does not alter a room's colors. In the evening, light becomes increasingly blue, so you may want to counteract this with warm, rich shades. Remember, too, that artificial light will cast a slightly yellow tone over the colors you have chosen.

The best way to test the suitability of a color is to paint a patch on a large piece of cardboard and observe it in different parts of the room, at different times of the day, and in different qualities of light.

## Special effects and special paints

The way you apply color is also important. To introduce gentle color, you could decorate a wall with a less intense, nonuniform finish – perhaps by stippling, ragging, sponging, or distressing. These techniques all diffuse the color without diluting the shade itself. A more intense effect can be achieved by colorwashing (building up many layers of diluted paint to give a greater depth of color), or by using lacquer to add a wonderful shine that reflects the light. Many traditional paints, such as milk-based pigments and distempers, offer subtle ways to color your home.

● Green paint with a hint of yellow makes this attic bedroom seem inviting.

● Bold primaries – deep reds, strong blues, bright greens, and sunny yellows – inject vitality.

● Various shades of white on different surfaces make a fascinating decorative scheme for a bedroom (right). Instead of relying on color, the room is designed around the contrasting textures of painted and distressed wood, stone, and natural fabrics. A rich gold-embroidered fabric panel on the canopy gives a touch of opulence, and a charcoal-painted molding around the ceiling adds definition. A blue-and-white bathroom (opposite) could easily be cold, but the creamy off-white tones of the tiles and woodwork add welcome warmth.

# white

With its associations of innocence, cleanliness, and purity, white creates peaceful and relaxing interiors. On the face of it, white is easy to use because it mixes well with all sorts of colors, seems to enlarge small spaces, brightens dark rooms, and, when used as a traditional whitewash either inside the home or out, conjures up simple country style. But the old-fashioned whitewashes and distempers are a far cry from the brilliant-white paints so widely available these days. They had an almost dusty texture, which gave an altogether softer result and created a very different effect as they yellowed with age.

*"The whitewash'd wall, the nicely sanded floor. The varnished clock that ticked behind the door."*

OLIVER GOLDSMITH

Pure white paint that does not discolor with age is a relatively modern invention. It has a bluish tint and is most effective when there is lots of strong, natural light. In Greece and other Mediterranean countries, for instance, pure whites look resplendent in the sunshine against the vivid background of blue sea and sky. But in less intense light they can seem rather cold and stark, and instead of aging with charm to give a lived-in feel, they can quickly look rather dirty and dingy.

The answer is to use white paint to which a dash of pigment has been added. A hint of red, yellow, or brown results in a slightly creamy, warm white that has all the freshness of pure white, but none of the harshness. A hint of black produces a silvery gray-tinted white that gives the impression of a serene, misty sky.

## White facts
Things to think about when choosing white

**Natural whites**
Snow, doves, swans, clouds, pearl, chalk, marble, milk

**Symbolism**
Innocence, purity, cleanliness, peace, serenity

**Use in the home**
Muslin, cotton, linen, pickled floors, whitewashed walls, porcelain, altar candles

● White rooms need to be bathed in plenty of light, so windows are left bare in this elegant living room (opposite, above). Simple decorating schemes are perfect for creating peaceful areas in which you can read or just relax (opposite, below). If you choose pickled floorboards and sparse furnishings nothing will distract your attention. In rooms where you want white walls to give an unadorned look (left), furniture and flooring should have the same feel – natural matting, painted furniture, linen upholstery, muslin shades, and fresh flowers all have natural simplicity.

In these instances, the amount of color added is so tiny that the white keeps its luminosity, but takes on a whole new character.

Interiors that use these subtle off-whites look most striking when everything else is as pared down as the color palette. Clear of clutter and relying instead on the texture of natural materials such as wood, stone, and unbleached fabrics, these rooms are conducive to concentration, clarity of thought, rest, and relaxation.

An accent of color against such a backdrop – a vase of vibrant flowers, a painting, or some jewel-colored accessories – will have great impact. Alternatively, opt for a striking monochrome look and introduce black accessories or, for a touch of classic elegance, try gilded furniture, which looks wonderful against the warmer whites, and gives an understated richness that is never too showy.

# blue

*"Blue colour is everlastingly appointed by the Deity to be a source of delight."*

JOHN RUSKIN

● A dreamy pale-blue and white scheme creates a perfect, restful bedroom (far left). Wood, wicker, and shades of pink in the flowers and furnishings add a touch of warmth (left). A sky-blue staircase recedes into the distance (below).

## Blue facts
Things to think about when choosing blue

**Complementary color**
Orange

**Natural blues**
Sky, water, cobalt, aquamarines, sapphires, bachelor's buttons

**Symbolism**
Infinity, calm, melancholy, relaxation, coolness, tranquility

**Use in color therapy**
Reducing blood pressure and inflammation

Blue rooms are incredibly peaceful – just imagining sky blue somehow makes everything seem calmer and more relaxed. Perhaps it's because this ethereal color conjures up endless summer skies and vast oceans, or because soft blues are undemanding on the eye (blue is, after all, a receding color). Whatever the reason, blue is arguably the most spiritual color of the spectrum.

Blues can also be rich and vibrant. Much depends on whether the paint has a strong, warm base with touches of cobalt or ultramarine, or a cooler one, reminiscent of indigo. Bright blues can look stunning on their own, but they often need a touch of white to stop them being too overpowering.

More tranquil options include powder blue, a gentle, cool shade best used in rooms with plenty of natural light and combined with lots of white; lavender gives a calming country feel, its pinkish tones adding warmth; duck-egg blue is refreshing and unobtrusive; aquamarine serene; and gray-blue evokes 18th-century Gustavian style from Scandinavia.

Too many shades of blue used together can look a little cold and uninviting, however, so take advantage of the fact that blue is a good mixer, especially with white. For harmony, combine blues with closely related colors in similar tones – you could match dusty blue with pale green, sandy yellow, or pale mauve, for example. To lift a stronger blue, add a touch of orange, bright green, or warm egg-yolk yellow. To turn up the heat, introduce wood and terra cotta, whose orange tones bring complementary accents and warmth in a subtle, natural way.

*"How lush and lusty the grass looks!*
*How green."*

WILLIAM SHAKESPEARE

● Strong, dark green is a striking choice for a small bedroom (far left). White bed linen and touches of complementary red in an antique patchwork bedspread make the effect cozy rather than overpowering. Green is also a good choice for this living room (left), which uses different shades on walls and woodwork for a harmonious result.

# green

Associated with freshness and springtime, green is perfect for creating a natural, restful, and secure environment. A touch of green in your home will have much the same cheering effect as seeing new leaves and shoots after a long winter. Greens blend well together and combine successfully with most other colors.

From turquoise, emerald, apple green, and acid lime to soft olive, sage, pistachio, and forest green, all are welcoming. Some greens are neutral, too, seeming neither to advance nor recede, and are useful for creating rooms with a restrained mood. Red can jazz up green's natural subtlety.

## Green facts
Things to think about when choosing green

**Complementary color**
Red

**Natural greens**
Vegetation, emeralds

**Symbolism**
Freshness, jealousy, innocence, harmony, reassurance, peace

**Use in color therapy**
General calm and well-being

For a simple effect, opt for soft, light sage or pistachio. These greens include lots of white and look good with all the neutrals, pale pinks, and soft golds. Add a touch of cherry red for a folk-art feel. Bright apple greens are evocative of the Caribbean and the Mediterranean, and are wonderful with strong blues, yellows, and pinks. Lime green, teamed with other citrus shades and plenty of white, injects vitality.

Strong, darker bottle greens are more dramatic and give sumptuous results when used alongside rich reds, oranges, dark pinks, and deep yellows. Dusty olives and browner greens look good with wood and terra cotta, and are perfect for natural, uncomplicated decorating schemes that reflect the Shaker tradition of simplicity.

# yellow

*"You have yellow walls – so have I;*
*yellow is the colour of joy."*

OSCAR WILDE

Wherever it is used, yellow will lift the spirits. Most of its positive associations come from the fact that yellow is the color of sunshine. It reminds us of spring flowers and transports us to hotter climates.

The brightest color in the spectrum, yellow can be either hot or cold, depending on the amount of red it contains. Egg-yolk yellow and butter yellow are rich and warm; lemon yellow has a more acid tinge; and ocher is earthy and mellow. Whatever shade you choose, yellow is a color that enhances natural light, so it works well in rooms that are usually dark or chilly.

Strong, warm yellow can be quite commanding because of its sheer vitality and because the colors that you will need to place with it must be just as powerful. Team it with vibrant pinks, blues, and greens rather than softer pastels, as these will look drab beside it. White is a good partner and can help to diffuse some of the heat. Primrose yellow creates a more peaceful effect and is also more versatile as it sits happily alongside cool blues, lavenders, and grays.

## Yellow facts
Things to think about
when choosing yellow

**Complementary color**
Violet

**Natural yellows**
Sun, sunflowers,
daffodils, gold

**Symbolism**
Happiness, heat, energy

**Use in color therapy**
Warming and
stimulating the body

● Warm yellow, tempered with lots of white and wood, makes a cheerful, welcoming dining room that seems sunny whatever the weather.

44

*"O, my Luve's like a red, red rose*
*That's newly sprung in June."*

ROBERT BURNS

# red

● The natural reds in bare wood and terra-cotta tiles inspired the subtle red paint shades used in these rooms. The color takes on a Shaker look when accented with rustic furniture and matching window frames (left), but creates a more refined country style when teamed with delicate furniture, china, and patterned flooring (below).

With its powerful primitive associations and sense of passion and daring, red can be a difficult color to live with in large amounts. Nevertheless, red interiors can be wonderfully rich and rewarding. You don't have to paint a wall crimson to take advantage of this palette either – use just a touch of red here and there, or choose a related shade that is less forceful, and you'll soon see how it can bring warmth and softness to your home.

Soft reds often play such a subtle part in a room's decoration that you hardly notice that they are there; their presence in terra cotta, wood, wicker, or stone often contributes a richness to the room's overall design scheme without being strident. Adobe pink, russet, and terra cotta all have a natural, autumnal feel that complements blue, green, white, and gold. Such warm red-browns have been used in interiors for centuries, their earthy pigments always cheap and easily available. Perhaps this is why rooms decorated in these shades seem timeless and universal.

Brighter, more striking reds, such as scarlet and raspberry, can be lovely when used in small amounts to create a folksy atmosphere. Alternatively, you can make the most of the warmth and inviting quality of strong, deep reds, by using them on the walls of cozy, enveloping rooms – a dining room, for example, will look dazzling by candlelight at night, and a bedroom or living room will seem enclosed and secure.

## Red facts
Things to think about when choosing red

**Complementary color**
Green

**Natural reds**
Rubies, poppies, roses, terra cotta, embers

**Symbolism**
Passion, anger, warmth, energy

**Use in color therapy**
Increasing heart rate and circulation

● Whitewashed walls, exposed beams, and a wooden floor accentuate the simple charm of this rustic bedroom (overleaf).

"*The deep, deep peace of the double bed after the hurly-burly of the chaise longue.*"

MRS. PATRICK CAMPBELL

● Neutral schemes work very well in minimalist interiors (this page), where everything from color to clutter is toned down. Texture is of primary importance in the simply decorated room (right), where the patterns inherent in the seagrass flooring, fabrics, baskets, pottery, and wood take the place of color.

# neutrals

Sophisticated in their restraint, neutral decorating schemes are perfect for quiet, contemplative spaces such as studies, living rooms, and bedrooms. They are extremely easy on the eyes and have a natural simplicity that is appealing to those who like their surroundings subdued, uncomplicated, and effortlessly stylish.

All neutrals, whether based on grays, browns, greens, or yellows, work well together as none is so strong that it detracts from another's subtlety. A limitless amount of variation on the neutral theme is therefore possible: choose from a mixture of the many shades of ivory, khaki, gray, cream, beige, stone, straw, buff, sand, biscuit, and many more.

Since all these colors are based on the naturally occurring tones found in the earth, in wood, and in stone, try to introduce these materials into a neutral interior to enhance its organic feel. Look for unpainted wooden furniture, pieces of earthenware and terra cotta, and beach finds such as driftwood and pebbles. Opt for wooden, terra-cotta, or stone floors, or choose seagrass matting or undyed wool carpets. Then add soft furnishings in muslin, gauze, and linen to complement the other elements.

Using these natural materials in conjunction with neutral paint shades also creates textural interest, which, together with a variety of tonal variations, is the key to making neutral rooms interesting instead of plain and dull. The pattern in seagrass matting, the variations in the clay of an earthenware pot, or the intricacy of wood grain offer a richness that more than compensates for the lack of color.

If you still yearn for some color, however, you'll find that a neutral decor provides the perfect background against which to introduce bright accents. Remember to keep the decorative elements simple, otherwise the effect will be lost. A bright pillow, a display of colorful ceramics, or one stunning fabric will be enough to lift the room out of the ordinary and bring it to life.

Whatever direction you choose, the joy of neutrals is that they will always seem fresh and uncontrived – the essence of a peaceful home.

● All neutrals work well with one another. In this
harmonious living room (opposite), many shades of beige,
cream, soft gold, and ivory sit happily together on walls,
upholstery, and floor. A vase of flowers instantly adds
interest to a neutral scheme (above).

# perspective

Color can be powerful, playing tricks on the eyes as well as the emotions. Just as certain colors in certain situations will seem to alter the proportions of a room, so they will change the way you perceive your house as a whole and the way the rooms relate to one another.

Hallways and corridors, where color schemes interact as they are glimpsed all together through open doors, are a useful place to start. Look into your house from the front door and consider what you see: it might be an unwelcoming space that doesn't appear to be connected to the rest of the house; or you might see a set of colors that seem to invite you to step into the hall, then into the rooms that open off it.

Using color as a link can make all the difference. You don't have to decorate the whole house in exactly the same color – choose just one element, such as the baseboards, dado, or flooring, as the unifying factor to lead the eye from the hall to the neighboring rooms and beyond. This can give your house a more relaxed, harmonious atmosphere. It also prevents the paint-box effect you often get – especially in small houses or apartments – when every room is decorated in a completely different palette.

Next, look at how the different colors you have used in adjoining rooms feed off one another, creating yet more optical illusions. A terra-cotta-colored wall seen through the door of a blue room will seem to come toward you, making the two areas appear closer together, whereas a pale-blue corridor will seem to stretch on forever. Paint the wall at the far end in a bright, warm color, however, and it will instantly seem less distant.

Be a little ingenious and make the colors you have chosen for your house work together to link or isolate rooms, to make spaces seem bigger or smaller, or to disguise or emphasize a certain feature – in other words, to create an environment that works for you and meets your needs.

● The glimpse of a fresh, apple-green wall grabs your attention. Only such a vibrant color could seem as eye-catching against the yellow walls of the hallway.

# mixing color

There are few rules to follow when mixing color, since it is largely a matter of taste. Just do what your instincts tell you, and if you like it and feel happy living with it, then it works. Sometimes, though, it's good to experiment and try something different – either more daring or more restrained than usual – and see what happens.

Thinking back to the color wheel (pages 34–35), you'll remember that complementary colors used together provide the strongest visual effects, and that adjoining colors create the most harmonious ones. There's no doubt that equal proportions of, say, yellow and purple, red and green, or orange and blue in a room would be quite hard to relax with. However, adding touches of one or the other of these colors will inject vibrancy and allow you to move away from safe and conventional single-color decorating schemes.

Dramatic color combinations are good if you are feeling dynamic and energetic. More peaceful, harmonious ones can be achieved by using similar shades of one color, or closely related colors of similar tone (try pinks and lilacs, or browns and creams). Whichever option you choose, before you start, make a color board, with patches of paint and swatches of fabric, to check that all the elements work well together and create the effect you want.

Many of the best color partnerships draw their inspiration from nature: imagine a sunflower against a summer sky, or moss on a stone wall. Others can be sparked by something already in the room, such as a fabric, a painting, or a rug. A color scheme might also be chosen to capture the essence of another country or to conjure up another era – a Victorian-style house might seem more at ease decorated in authentic deep reds, greens, and browns. Some color combinations are timeless, however. Blue and white, for example, have been used together in simple homes for centuries; the pairing often suggests nautical style.

Perhaps the hardest thing about mixing several colors in a room is knowing when to stop. Once you've been inspired by something, stick to the colors in that family – for example, all earth tones, all primaries, all pastels, or all historical paints – and your home will seem consistent and composed.

● Colors with the same tonal values work best together – soft red and lichen green are perfect partners (right). A stronger green needs to be combined with equally strong blues and yellows (overleaf).

● Add pattern to a room by choosing natural flooring such as wool, seagrass, and linoleum (above), or by introducing fabrics adorned with flower sprigs, stripes, and checks (opposite).

## Questions to ask when choosing pattern

● What adds pattern to your home – fabrics, wallcoverings, flooring, accessories, or natural textures?

● Do you feel more comfortable in plain or patterned rooms?

● Do you prefer patterns to be orderly or random, busy or subtle?

● Are you fond of traditional stripes, dots, ticking, or gingham?

● Would a floral pattern be an appropriate choice?

# looking at pattern

A room in which the walls, floor, furniture, and accessories all have plain surfaces of even, unbroken color would be cold, clinical, and soulless. Along with color and texture, pattern, no matter how subtle, is one of the most basic decorating requirements because it brings a room to life, adding character, depth, and visual interest.

## Introducing pattern

Fabrics, wallpapers, paint effects, and flooring, plus decorative items such as china or rugs, will all add pattern to a room. They don't have to be garish or brash, however – a fabric with a self-pattern or a sponged wall will give enough variation to excite the eye. Pattern can allow you to introduce a strong color to a room without having to take the plunge and use it everywhere. It is also a quick way to establish a mood – whether regular and orderly with a smart stripe, old-fashioned and countrified with a faded chintz, or flamboyant and spontaneous with a repeated hand-painted motif.

## Florals

Flower motifs are one of the most versatile and time-honored patterns, and are generally used to create a soft, romantic atmosphere. Chintz fabrics suit many different settings – from elegant drawing rooms to cozy country parlors. Small-scale spriggy florals, on fabrics and wallpapers, are synonymous with cottage style and look pretty in bedrooms. Toiles, depicting charming and idealized rural scenes, are another country-style favorite.

## Geometrics

Stripes and checks are both timeless classics. Translated to fabrics, these patterns have been used for centuries on ticking and gingham, and are still as popular as ever. They work extremely well with many florals, their simplicity acting as a good foil for more complex and intricate designs. Stripes can assume a more sophisticated role when used on wallpaper under a molding, for example, or on a larger scale as stylish upholstery fabric. Checkerboard and other geometric floors are another effective way of introducing pattern to a room. You could use tiles or simply paint a design straight onto the floor. The bold pattern and blocks of soft color on many ikat fabrics, although less obviously geometric, look striking in a variety of settings.

## Paint effects

Walls can be decorated with special paint effects to add understated pattern variation as well as subtle color. Ragging, stippling, or graining all create gentle backgrounds, but there's nothing to keep you from hand painting or stenciling stronger geometric designs on walls if you feel that the room can benefit from a more dominant pattern.

● Pattern is the main decorative element in this bedroom (left), where stripes and checks linked by color are used on the curtains, bedspread, and other accessories. Unusually patterned carpet squares (opposite) would add impact to a neutral scheme.

● Two bedrooms use pattern to create very different effects: a bold, hand-stenciled design makes one wall the focus of the room (left), while serene blue-and-white stripes and checks on walls, upholstery, and matting create a calm and restrained air (right).

# using pattern

A room filled with a lot of busy patterns is not usually conducive to peace and relaxation – it's too fussy and distracting. But used judiciously, amid blocks of plain color, pattern will attract the eye and focus the attention. A rich, patterned fabric or pretty wallpaper in the right setting will seem all the more beautiful.

You also need to consider where in the house to use pattern. A room that is always full of people and activity, or one where you tend to retreat for five minutes' quiet rest, is not the best place for a complex patterned wallpaper. In these settings, opt instead for just one splash of pattern, such as a boldly upholstered sofa or some jazzy pillows. Much depends on the pattern itself, of course. Uniform designs on fabrics and wallpapers are good for calmer spaces that need a sense of order, while free-flowing, asymmetrical patterns are best reserved for rooms where you want to feel energized.

Like color, pattern can play tricks on the eye. Scale is an important consideration here, since large patterns can advance and small ones recede, depending on their color. You could, therefore, use a large design to make an imposing room seem more intimate – a useful way to make you feel more at ease in a large space. Alternatively, you could add a geometric pattern on one wall to compensate for lack of regularity in an odd-shaped room, or try a small-scale print all over walls and ceiling to disguise awkward angles or a sloping roof.

Don't be afraid to mix patterns together to create a deliberately lush and distinctive environment. Make color the link between all the elements for greater impact. Just think of a traditional patchwork quilt and you'll realize how a myriad of patterns can work well together in the right context.

# displaying
## your collection

Some smooth pebbles picked up on vacation, a set of old leather-bound books, or a shelf lined with quirky teapots all reflect your personality as much as the way you decorate or furnish a room. A healthy number of treasured possessions is a good indication not just of your taste, but also of the fact that you are at home in your surroundings. They show that you have identified the good things in life. Your collections don't have to be expensive – it's their sentimental value that matters.

People are natural collectors – even those with minimalist interiors often have a penchant for a certain designer's furniture or a certain style of artwork. But when the magpie tendency takes hold and you find yourself with more spongeware pitchers than you can use just to arrange flowers, how should you display them? Choosing an unused cubby or an empty corner to show off your favorite things is half the fun.

You could place your collection on a mantel or a windowsill, install some corner shelves, mass bits and pieces on top of a chest, or hang them from a Shaker-style peg rack. Fragile pieces look even more precious under glass – search secondhand stores for a shadow-box frame, a glazed cabinet, or a glass-topped table with compartments underneath. An expanse of wall can be covered with baskets or plates instead of pictures, or you could do what generations have done before and fill the shelves of a hutch with row upon row of cups on hooks, piles of bowls, and handsome platters. Kitchen exhibits are always changing because the items are often in use. Coupled with ephemera – perhaps a postcard from a friend, some family photographs, or flowers from the backyard – these are among the most expressive and personal displays in the home.

● Kitchenware in all its forms can bring a room to life. Shelves laden with a casual assortment of dishes, pans, and gadgets (far right) are just as inviting as the more formal arrangement of a matching set of china (above). Uniform displays can be enlivened by introducing something new – pictures in gilt frames, for example, make white china seem even more pristine (right).

Traditional showcases, such as the china-laden hutch or the mantel with
its clock and candlesticks, are comforting and nostalgic. Other classic ways to
group objects include arranging things in threes, a configuration that is
naturally pleasing to the eye; placing together objects with such similar features
as color or texture; surrounding a collection with plenty of space so that each
item can "breathe"; and placing a mirror behind a group to double the
impression it creates.

But you don't have to follow any rules. In fact, unconventional ideas are
often the most eye-catching. Try mixing old with new, natural with
man-made, precious with frivolous, curves with angles. Be witty and let your
sense of fun run wild. The less contrived and the more idiosyncratic, the better.
And whatever eclectic collections you put on show, be sure to freshen up or even
change them from time to time – they'll alter a room's character in an instant.

● The most effective displays are often those with
a sense of unity. An array of basketware seen
en masse draws attention to the variety of textures
and patterns (opposite), while a line of richly colored
copper pans makes the other metallic surfaces in the
kitchen shine even more brightly (above).

# looking at lighting

Just as a room's atmosphere can be created by lighting, it can also be destroyed, no matter how imaginative and restful your choice of color, fabric, pattern, texture, or furnishings. If you plan lighting before you begin to decorate, instead of leaving it until the last minute, the results will be more harmonious.

Well-designed artificial lighting schemes are always a compromise between function and aesthetics, but anything that mimics the subtle and changeable qualities of natural light is a good choice for a relaxing room. Think how sunlight varies during the day and in different seasons, and how it differs when filtered by leaves, clouds, or mist – then you'll realize why a single bulb hanging in the center of a room is rarely the best option. Several variable and versatile light sources, carefully positioned for different purposes, work much better.

## A plan of action

Think about when the room is used most, what it is used for, and which furniture or decorative features you would like to highlight. Then opt for a mix of ambient lighting, task lighting, accent lighting, and decorative lighting.

Ambient lighting is the general background illumination provided, for example, by pendants, up- or downlighters, and wall sconces. All should be well shaded and subtly positioned so that their light floods the walls and ceiling. Task lighting illuminates specific activities, such as reading or cooking, and can be provided by halogen spotlights, desk lamps, floor lights, or well-shaded fluorescent strips. Accent lighting uses spots, picture lights, or strips in alcoves to pick out or enhance an interesting feature. Decorative lights, such as candelabras or chandeliers, are more about looks and mood-setting than practicality.

The more flexible your lighting scheme, the easier it will be to live with. A dimmer switch is invaluable, especially for

## Questions to ask when planning lighting

- Do you use the room for relaxing, reading, working, or socializing?
- How will you provide background illumination?
- Which areas need task lighting?
- What objects or features would you like to highlight?
- Which fixtures would suit your room scheme?
- Is your lighting flexible?
- How will light affect the room's colors and textures?
- Can you use lighting to make the room seem larger or cozier?

ambient lighting, as it will enable you to change the atmosphere from bright and practical to soft and restful. Directional flexibility is also an asset – for instance, an adjustable desk light that doubles as an uplighter.

Always shade a light source to avoid glare and hard-edged shadows. Pendant lights should be enclosed in spherical shades, and table lamps should be positioned so the bulb itself is not visible.

## Light and color

Different types of bulb emphasize different areas of the spectrum, and you can use this to your advantage when planning the overall room scheme. For soft yellow light use an ordinary tungsten bulb; for clear white light opt for low-voltage halogen; for a blue effect choose an energy-efficient fluorescent bulb. The color of the lampshade also alters the way you perceive paint hues, so try to choose one that complements your color scheme.

## A trick of the light

Perception of space, perspective, texture, and, ultimately, mood depends on lighting. A low-ceilinged room can be made to appear more open by directing lights upward, an imposing one made more intimate by training them down. A more spacious feel can be achieved by flooding walls that are opposite each other with light or by placing a light source in front of a mirror. Shiny surfaces, such as metal, silky fabrics, and polished wood, reflect light, so they need careful treatment to avoid seeming harsh. Natural wood, matte fabrics, and stone, however, absorb light and can seem to disappear without the appropriate amount of lighting. It's also worth remembering that shadows can throw textures into relief, adding a touch of drama.

## Style is everything

Fixtures and lampshades should always blend in with the rest of the room. Choose hi-tech lighting for modern and minimalist interiors, iron or verdigris bases for a more rustic look, glass-drop chandeliers for grand statements, sconces for elegance, and oil lamps for period style.

● Lamps can be used for gentle ambient lighting as well as to illuminate specific activities such as reading. Try to include several different light sources in each room for maximum flexibility.

69

● White-painted surfaces and white fabrics intensify the light that enters this bedroom window (far left). In rooms that get plenty of sun (left), you can afford to have dark-colored window frames and darker pieces of furniture. To make the most of natural light, keep window treatments simple (overleaf).

# natural light

When planning a comfortable and uplifting home, natural light sources are an important consideration; think how depressing it is to be deprived of daylight in winter, and how your spirits lift instantly with the arrival of spring sun. Houses that let in plenty of light are also more in tune with the natural world, as the people inside are aware of the time of day, the season, and the weather.

If possible, choose a room's function according to the quality of sunlight it receives. A bedroom or a breakfast room should enjoy the morning sun, while a dining room that is flooded with sun in the evening is instantly convivial. Use rooms that receive the least sunshine as utility rooms and storerooms. If it's not possible to plan your house like this, maximize the amount of natural light that enters each room by choosing simple window treatments, especially ones that can be tied back during the day. Try not to clutter up windowsills, and be sure to cut back plants that may grow over the window in summer. Introduce shiny surfaces, mirrors, and lots of warm-tinted white paint to reflect the extra light you have gained.

Too much sunlight, however, can sometimes make a room uncomfortably hot and glaringly bright. Use shutters or blinds to block out the rays, or choose curtains made from sheer fabric or lace. These will diffuse the light and fill the room with a bright but less intense glow.

"And I shall have some peace there,
for peace comes dropping slow,
Dropping from the veils of the
morning to where the cricket sings."

W.B. YEATS

# using lighting

When it comes to planning lighting around the home, the living room usually has the most complex needs. It is used for many different tasks – reading, socializing, children's games, watching television, eating – and each has to be accommodated. An adaptable combination might include a floor lamp beside an armchair, making a comfortable place to read, uplighters to wash the walls with a relaxing glow, and several movable and adjustable lamps to fulfill a variety of additional requirements.

Try to plan so that each light, or group of lights, can be operated separately. This is especially useful if you have a combined living and dining room; clever lighting can differentiate each area, creating two rooms out of one. When the meal is over, simply turn off the lights above the table and illuminate the room's seating area.

In dining rooms, candles, hurricane lamps, and decorative lighting such as chandeliers come into their own. A light that is suspended over a table should be positioned quite low to avoid dazzling the diners. Soft, relaxing light is essential in bedrooms, along with task lights for reading, while a child's room may need the reassuring glow of a nightlight.

Clever task lighting is also essential in kitchens, bathrooms, and studies. Halogen lighting is a good option for spotlights above kitchen surfaces and the sink, for a desk light in a study, and for clear illumination in the bathroom. To light the bathroom mirror, the beam should be directed at the person using it, not at the mirror itself.

● Three approaches to dining-room lighting: a simple candelabra (right above) gives a soft, warm light in a wood-filled country room; two modern adjustable pendants provide soft pools of light at each end of a refectory table (right below); and elegant hurricane lamps create a sophisticated focus for a formal gathering (far right).

# candlelight

Soft, flickering candlelight is romantic and atmospheric, providing the perfect finishing touch to a dining table, a late-evening summer garden party, an afternoon by the fire, or a sensuous bathtime soak. Candles are so calming that they are indispensable to the peaceful home.

A candle may give a less powerful light than an electric bulb, but its effect on a room's mood is far more potent. Candles look striking in isolation, stunning en masse. The flame of a single altar candle surrounded by a sculpture of wax droplets can be mesmerizing; so, too, is a row of candles above the fireplace, intensifying the image of the hearth as the brightest and warmest part of the room. Try filling small containers with tea lights and dot them around the room like stars, or float small, wide candles among flower petals in a dish of water at the center of the table. Beeswax candles are wonderful as they have a distinctive, old-fashioned scent.

Hurricane lamps and storm lanterns give a heartwarming glow whatever the weather – there's something primitive and comforting about their dancing flames on a wild and blustery night. Any naked flame, in fact, will bring out the best in a room full of mirrors, multiplying its magical light and adding to the sense of relaxation.

● Candles look very effective when they are grouped together. They are the *pièce de résistance* of an alfresco meal on the terrace (right); and small votive lights in a variety of containers form a striking, tiered arrangement on the staircase (left).

# festivals of light

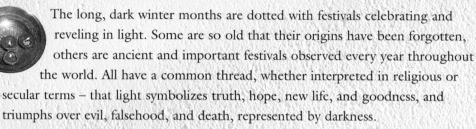

The long, dark winter months are dotted with festivals celebrating and reveling in light. Some are so old that their origins have been forgotten, others are ancient and important festivals observed every year throughout the world. All have a common thread, whether interpreted in religious or secular terms – that light symbolizes truth, hope, new life, and goodness, and triumphs over evil, falsehood, and death, represented by darkness.

On a moonless night in October or November, Hindus celebrate Diwali, which means "garland of lights" and is held in honor of Lakshmi, goddess of prosperity and fortune. She will enter only houses that have no dark corners, so as night descends, hundreds of lights – called diwas – are lit all over the house as well as in temples, shops, and offices. Fireworks light up one of the darkest skies of the year – a symbol for new beginnings and hope for the future.

The Jewish eight-day festival of Chanukah, celebrated in November or December, commemorates a miracle that took place 2,000 years ago during the Maccabean rededication of the Temple in Jerusalem. When the perpetual lamp was about to be lit, there was only enough oil for it to burn for one day, yet it lasted for eight. This is celebrated by lighting one light on the first day of Chanukah, two on the second, and so on, until all eight are burning.

Ancient pagan festivals used fire to celebrate fertility and encourage the return of spring. Many of these

● Lighted candles are central to Christmas, a festival that occurs at a time of the year when many ancient cultures celebrated the lengthening days (left and opposite). The flickering flame creates a magical effect, but care should always be taken when placing candles near flammable materials.

An arrangement of candles will enhance any festive occasion (opposite and below) and a mirror provides the perfect backdrop for an eclectic display (right). At the Hindu festival of light, Diwali, gifts of sweetmeats decorated with silver paper are exchanged and shared among friends and family (above).

customs, such as the burning of logs and candles at the Vikings' Yuletide feast, are now part of the Christian festivals of Christmas and Candlemas, in which candles symbolize Christ as "the light of the world." Pre-Christian symbolism also coexists in Christmas traditions such as setting light to the the plum pudding – an image of the sun. In Sweden, the celebrations held on December 13 for the martyred Christian Saint Lucia take the form of processions led by young girls whose crowns of lighted candles welcome the lengthening of the days and look forward to the melting of the ice.

The festivities of the winter solstice in the United States and northern Europe are also a time to remember the dead. On Halloween night, also called All Souls' Eve, lanterns made from pumpkins or turnips are set on doors and windows to ward off evil spirits. In Finland lighted candles are placed on family graves every Christmas Eve.

The coming of the New Year is also celebrated with light; numerous communities the world over have their own rituals, which include everything from carrying flaming torches or barrels of burning tar to lighting bonfires. Paper lanterns also mark the New Year celebrations in both Japan and China.

Few symbols are as universal or as potent as fire and light, and the festivals that celebrate them hold a special meaning for you, wherever you live and whatever your beliefs.

# touch

There should be something in every room that invites you to reach out and touch – rough or smooth, hard or soft, shiny or matte, fine or coarse. It could be a piece of gnarled driftwood, a polished surface, a water-worn pebble, a velvet pillow, a cool marble statue, a wood-fired pot, a handwoven fabric, some sensuous silk, or a downy quilt. All these glorious textures give a room comforting contrasts.

Traditional, naturally textured materials such as raw cotton, wood, and stone bring life to the simplest and most sparsely decorated interiors and are valued as much for their feel as for their appearance or color. Surface texture also lends character – possessions that are old, worn, battered, scratched, or dented often possess more charm than things that are pristine.

For a rich and rewarding environment, fill your home with all manner of tactile pleasures.

● Contrast is the key to tactile displays – the different properties of terra cotta, wood, wicker, ceramics, plants, and leaves combine to form a wonderful tapestry of textures.

# choosing texture

At first glance, the textures in a room might not be as obvious as colors or patterns, but they have an important role to play, especially in houses that are designed to appeal to the senses. While some textures can be quite striking – a smooth expanse of marble or an opulent length of velvet – others have to be examined closely to be appreciated fully. You might have to run a piece of silk through your fingers to enjoy its quality or walk barefoot on a stone floor to feel its gentle undulations.

Fabrics, furniture, flooring, and decorative objects all bring a wonderful range of textures to home interiors. Smooth, hard, shiny surfaces reflect the light and create a bright, fresh, stimulating environment that can be businesslike and urbane – think of using polished wood, slate, marble, metal, linoleum, vitrified ceramics, glass, gloss paints, silky and dressed fabrics, and glass. Coarse, matte materials have warm, comforting, and relaxing properties, and include unpolished wood, limestone, distemper, rustic tiles, cork, natural flooring such as sisal, seagrass, and coir, raw cottons and linens, and fabrics including tweed, chenille, and wool.

You could introduce a predominance of textures from either of these groups to give your home a particular ambience, but it's always worth remembering that too many smooth, shiny elements together can seem hard and clinical, while too many rough ones might look dull. The key is to have some degree of contrast – think of a chenille throw over a leather sofa, or a gleaming metal stove in a stone-floored country kitchen.

Textural interest is crucial in rooms where there are no bright colors and where other decorative touches are kept to a minimum. In neutral schemes, different tactile elements may be the only source of contrast and variety – you might not notice the weave of a sisal floor covering in a room ablaze with color and pattern, but beside off-white walls and muslin curtains its intricate texture will be obvious and all the more welcoming.

● The tablecloth, curtains, and upholstery in this living room (opposite) offer an array of comforting textures, while glass on the table, mirror, and pictures adds contrasting, reflective accents. Conversely, in a hall with a polished wooden floor, a metal light fixture, and shiny gloss paint (right), an uneven, distressed paint finish on the chest introduces warmth and textural variety.

● Comfort and practicality should be your priority, so choose sofas, armchairs, and footstools that invite a mood of deep relaxation (this page and opposite).

## Questions to ask before choosing furniture

● What style do you want your furniture to set?

● Can you adapt existing pieces with new upholstery, a coat of paint, or different accessories?

● Is there at least one really comfortable piece of furniture in the room?

● Can the room be pared down and what's left made to look more attractive?

● Is there one item that can become the focal point of the room?

# looking at furniture

Furniture is extremely expressive. It defines your home's style and gives it special character. It also has an important part to play in something far more basic and more central to a peaceful home – comfort.

A sofa that looks sensational, or one that costs the earth, will not necessarily be more comfortable than one you buy in a secondhand store. Indeed, few people are able to fill their homes with costly or beautiful pieces of furniture. They have to supplement the things they already have with whatever they can pick up inexpensively, adapting or arranging them for a pleasant setting. There is always a degree of compromise, but if you make comfort and practicality your priority by choosing things you feel at home with, you can't go wrong.

## Setting style and mood

Particular pieces of furniture will instantly re-create certain styles – avant-garde, retrospective, or a look associated with another country. Be singleminded about what you are aiming for, and comb shops and markets for pieces of furniture that will work well together.

A favorite choice for calm and restful interiors is an old-fashioned look that recaptures the essence of a less stressful age. You can create elegant period rooms or informal rustic ones by adding a few well-chosen pieces of country-style furniture. Simple wooden items, either in their natural state or painted and distressed, can be blissfully easy to live with. Alternatively, if the sleek, uncomplicated lines of modern furniture are in tune with your desire for clutter-free living, seek out pieces in pale wood, plastic, glass, or metal.

Rather than having one uniform style throughout the house, you might consider changing it from room to room. This allows you to have some areas furnished with the family and relaxation in mind – an old pine table and chairs in the kitchen, a comfortable sofa in the living room, and a battered toy box in the playroom. Meanwhile, other rooms could be furnished for a more sophisticated look – a polished mahogany table in the dining room, a hand-carved desk in the study, or a dreamy four-poster in the bedroom. Mix and match to create whatever look works best in each room.

## Where to buy
Secondhand stores, flea markets, auctions, and antique shops are good sources for furniture with character and historical interest; these are often the pieces that keep their charm over the years, whereas contemporary ones can sometimes soon look dated. Look out for inexpensive items that can be given new life with a coat of paint or replacement hardware such as knobs, handles, or feet. Some new fabric – a few pillows, a throw, or a tablecloth, for instance – can give your chairs, tables, cupboards, or shelves an instant lift.

## Comfort zone
You need to choose beds, sofas, and chairs carefully. Take your time when buying these items, and make sure they feel as wonderful as they look: lie on a bed, sprawl on a sofa, and flop into a chair before you give it a home. Keep an eye out for such pieces as a rocking chair, a chaise longue, a day bed, or a reclining steamer chair – these are things people tend to make a beeline for in a room.

Be practical, too. Make sure that tables will easily seat the whole family plus guests, check that desks are a comfortable height to work at, and that chests really are big enough to store your clothes.

## Arranging furniture
Try to achieve a balance of items in every room – some decorative, some practical; some sociable, some solitary; some large, some small. Arrange groups of furniture within each room to reflect the needs of the people who use it, but try not to cram in too much – give your treasured pieces plenty of breathing space.

● A sophisticated living room uses a combination of painted and wooden furniture plus soft paint colors and gently draped fabric at the windows to conjure up elegant 18th-century style.

# choosing shapes

If you were buying a table, would the perfect design be round or square? Although there are practical considerations either way – a rectangular one has a space for the head of the table, a round one is perhaps more sociable – it's also a matter of aesthetics. Some people just like some shapes better than others.

Notice which shapes appear on the furniture and fabrics you are drawn to. There might be a number of circles and gentle curves, a series of sharp angles and straight lines, a repeated geometric motif, or lots of decorative twists and turns. Harmonious room schemes often have a mix of several of these elements, as curves make angles appear more gentle, while straight lines link circles and give an impression of order.

Furniture designed with lots of flowing curves often seems more relaxing and informal. If you agree, look for such living-room furniture as sofas and chairs that combine physical comfort with rounded shapes. Use other elements in the room – occasional tables, mirrors, pictures, rugs, and lighting – either to introduce more of the same shapes or to add a note of diversity.

Creating a sequence of similar shapes in a room is a good way of bringing a sense of cohesion to a scheme that doesn't seem to hang together properly. Pick out one strong, existing shape and build on it – in a bathroom, a sink with rounded corners could be echoed by the shape of a mirror above; in a kitchen, the curved molding on an antique cabinet could become the template for a decorative detail on a new shelf; in a bedroom, the design of a paisley bedspread could inspire a hand-painted border motif.

● Balanced shapes create harmonious rooms. The elegant angles of an armoire (opposite) are offset by the smooth curves of the chair and the bold shapes in the curtains and rug. Similarly, the straight lines of the table and chairs (below left) are balanced by the curved chair backs and the mirror. The intricate shape of the table legs forms a visual link with the pattern of the rug (below). The fluid, tapered lines of the bed are echoed in the tables and lamps (overleaf).

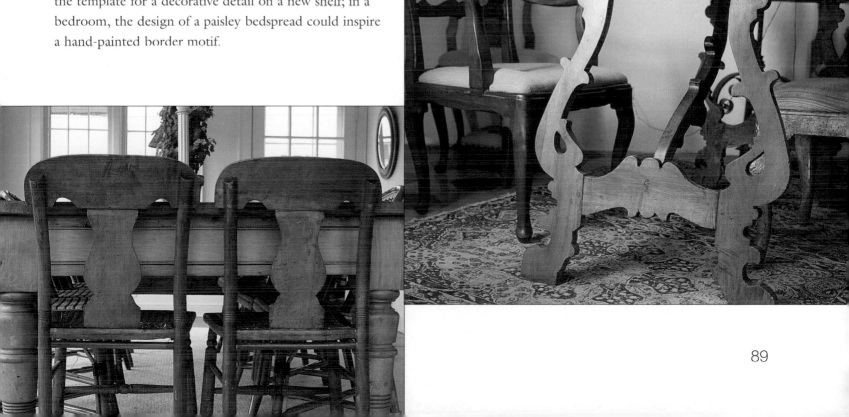

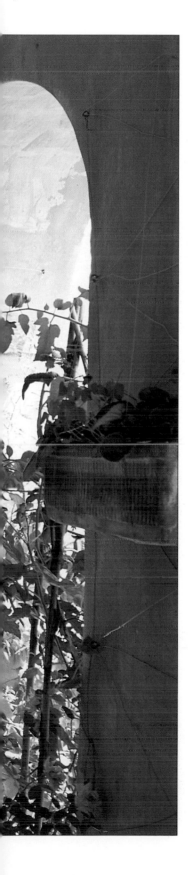

# outdoors in

All houses need some link with nature – even if it is just some container plants by the front door or a small paved area at the back with space for a table and chairs. For city dwellers, houseplants and windowboxes will lift the spirits. If, however, you have a proper garden room – an indoor conservatory, an outdoor terrace, or even a small glass-enclosed sun porch – you'll be able to experience the joy of having a place that blurs the boundaries between outdoors and indoors, somewhere for the healing, relaxing power of plants to work their magic.

Green is one of the most tranquil colors, and an abundance of foliage will promote well-being and transform a garden room into a sanctuary. On a more practical level, plants also oxygenate the environment, raise its humidity levels, and sometimes even purify the air.

Terraces, balconies, courtyards, porches, sunrooms, decks, and verandas are all flexible living spaces that can be used as informal outdoor dining rooms, play rooms, or places for rest and contemplation. They are perfect for days when it's too cold to be outside but too pleasant to be indoors.

Patios and verandas need to be situated in a position that catches the sun at the right time of day, yet has enough shade or dappled light to be comfortable

● An outdoor room furnished with a traditional cane table and chairs is the perfect place to sit and relax (left). In this large, airy sunroom (above), dining becomes a treat for the senses.

when temperatures rise. A parasol or a canopy of vines could be the answer. Balconies and decks also require some shelter from the wind. For sunrooms, you'll need adequate ventilation and simple canvas shades to provide protection from the elements. Plants – and humans, too – will bask in the comfort of their own little ecosystem.

Furnish your garden room with relaxing chairs – stylish, practical pieces could include deck chairs, director's chairs, rocking chairs, wicker chairs, hammocks, and even a daybed or chaise longue. You'll also need a table – wrought-iron or marble-topped café tables are both sturdy and pretty.

● House and garden merge on a cool and peaceful veranda in the shade of mature trees (left). Traditional wrought-iron furniture and simply planted containers add to the tranquility. A flourishing courtyard (above) means that city dwellers can also enjoy the benefits of an outdoor room.

Plants can be grouped on staging or shelving to display greenery at different heights. Old metal racks and spare bookshelves can be commandeered for use in your garden room, any chipped paint or rusty finish quickly disguised by foliage. Use a variety of containers for planting: As well as terra-cotta pots, jardinières, troughs, and garden urns, use baskets, barrels, galvanized buckets, old tins, enamelware, and porcelain sinks. If space permits, you could consider installing a small fountain to bring the alluring sound of gently trickling water to your garden room.

● Take a siesta on the daybed in this small sunroom (below), where the tall yuccas provide some shade and add architectural interest. Natural materials are good choices for garden rooms; lots of stone imparts warmth (right) and basket chairs are perfect for this sunny dining area (overleaf). The pots of lavender produce a glorious scent.

# working from home

Whether you run a business from home or simply need a small desk for writing letters and storing documents, your workspace should be comfortable, well equipped, and well planned. More and more people are shunning conventional office life, aware that working from home can be more rewarding and a good deal less stressful, so it is important not to undermine this change for the better by trying to function in a cramped, noisy, or unsympathetic space. You are likely to spend a lot of time here, and to avoid hazards such as headaches, back problems, and repetitive strain injury, it's essential that the conditions for your comfort are right. There's no reason why a home office shouldn't be as peaceful and mood-enhancing as any other part of your home.

Choose somewhere that is quiet and large enough for all your equipment and storage needs. This could be a study, a corner of another room, an alcove in a hallway, a converted attic, or even a shed in the backyard. It's a bonus to have somewhere that gets plenty of natural light so you won't have to resort to harsh fluorescent lighting. You'll need good ambient lighting for winter afternoons and evening work, plus task lighting – an adjustable desk light that is positioned above your desk where it casts no shadows on your work. Place the light slightly to the left if you are right-handed, just to the right if you are left-handed.

Make sure that your chair and desk are both comfortable and appropriate for the tasks you will be doing. Try to include a few work surfaces at different levels (typing requires a lower surface than writing, for instance) and consider investing in an adjustable office chair to encourage good posture and provide lumbar support.

● An old wooden table and chair are ideally positioned in front of the window (opposite), so when you take a break you can focus on the view and give your eyes and mind a well-earned rest. A long pine table clear of any clutter makes an elegant writing desk (right).

● A successful home office should always blend in comfortably with the rest of the house (opposite). In addition to a desk and office chair, it's a good idea to include some relaxing seating in your workspace (left). A small alcove under a sloping roof is an ideal place to slot in a small desk (above).

If you use a computer, make sure the desk is deep enough for both keyboard and monitor to be in front of you rather than to one side, which can cause neck strain. You might also like to invest in a foot rest and a wrist rest. Take regular breaks and try to relax as you work.

Depending on your budget and the style you would like your workroom to have, you could opt for a purpose-built modern desk, an antique one, or just a simple table. A separate room means you can distance yourself – physically and emotionally – from your work, but if your office is in the corner of another room, invest in a screen or a large rolltop desk so that you don't have to look at piles of unfinished work in the evening.

Clutter is not conducive to peace of mind, so keep your surroundings neat and orderly. Use storage boxes for odds and ends, baskets for filing papers, and old trunks and chests for material you don't refer to often. Keep important memos and clippings on a bulletin board, and remember to add a few inspiring postcards or family photographs.

● Fabrics with a self-pattern such as slubbed silk, cotton piqué, and taffeta (above) give subtle color and textural variation, while woven designs make a bolder statement (opposite).

## Questions to ask before choosing fabric

● Will the fabric get heavy use or is it just for show?

● Would a plain, natural fabric be best?

● Would a colored or patterned fabric be more appropriate?

● Do the colors harmonize with other elements in the room?

● Will the colors fade?

● Is the fabric washable?

● Is the fabric fire-retardant?

# looking at fabric

Fabrics bring comfort, color, pattern, texture, warmth, privacy, and decoration to a room. They also help to soften walls, floor, and furniture, making your surroundings more snug and intimate. Buying fabric can be an expensive business, however. The secret is to be liberal with cheaper options such as muslin and cotton, and to use smaller quantities of the more expensive fabrics.

To make sure the fabrics you are considering create the effect you want, include some scraps on a sample board along with patches of paint and swatches of floor covering. Fabric can often be a successful bridge between other colors in a room, or it can introduce something quite different – a splash of complementary color, for example, or a color accent in an otherwise neutral room scheme.

## Natural fabrics

Linen has a lovely texture and looks wonderful either dyed or undyed. Cotton is cheap and versatile; choose any weight from gauzy organdy to heavy denim or canvas, depending on where you intend to use it. Wool is a warm, insulating, soundproofing, and hard-wearing choice. Lighter, cooler, and more delicate, silk is available in various weights and is useful because it has a soft sheen and drapes well in luxurious folds.

## Patterned fabrics

Fabrics with a woven pattern range from opulent and heavy to simple and light. For a rich, warm effect, choose from self-colored damask, highly patterned brocade, heavy embroidered tapestry, decorative crewelwork, and colorful and sturdy tartan plaid. Lighter options include delicate lace, jaunty gingham, and traditional ticking. Fabrics that have a printed design include, among others, chintz, which is often polished to give a light sheen, toiles and Provençal fabrics.

## Sheer delight

Gauzy organdy and voile are perfect for filtering light as
well as for providing privacy. Hung in generous folds at a
window or around a bed they create a dreamy, floaty effect.
These fabrics can be either plain or patterned, and are
available in shades of white or cream, or in many colors.

## Window dressing

From simple café curtains to rich drapes with swags and
cascades, window treatments let you use fabric expressively.
Consider the shape of the window and the amount of light
you want to allow in, and then choose fabrics that match
the room's character. For a formal, tailored look, choose
full-length curtains, perhaps with neat headings, a valance,
and tasseled tiebacks. Suitable fabrics for such grand
statements are silks, brocades, and velvets. Lighter cottons,
such as gingham and muslin, look best – either floor-length
or sill-length – teamed with a simple wrought-iron or
wooden pole. For a really informal look, experiment with
lengths of a favorite fabric, a throw, sari material, or a sheet
casually draped over a pole.

## Fabric around the house

Bedrooms are a good place to indulge yourself with a
variety of fabrics made into bedhangings, dust ruffles,
canopies, covers, and pillows. Suspend sheer fabric from a
hoop to make a canopy that is reminiscent of a mosquito
net. In the bathroom, select fabrics such as toweling and
canvas that can deal with steam and moisture. Similarly, in
kitchens, choose simple preshrunk cottons for curtains and
tablecloths. Slipcovers are versatile and practical on
armchairs, dining chairs, and sofas. Made in linens and
muslin – which you could even dye yourself – they give
living rooms a relaxed air. For added comfort, and an
accent of color, scatter pillows made from scraps of
luxurious, more costly fabrics.

    With clever planning you could have two fabric schemes
in each room – one for winter that uses curtains, slipcovers
and pillows in heavier, darker colors, and one for summer
that makes the most of paler, thinner fabrics.

● Different patterns, weights, and textures are used on the dust ruffle,
bedcover, pillows, throws, and tablecloth to rich effect.

# textured
# fabrics

Introduce a wealth of texture to a room with fabrics. Velvet upholstery will enhance the softness of a sofa; a shimmering, slubbed silk curtain will draw attention to an attractive window; and crisp, white linen will make a bed seem more inviting.

For fabrics with a slight sheen, choose satin, silk, taffeta, and moiré. Use them as curtains and throws that will catch the light and offset undressed stone, brick, or wood to stunning effect. Traditionalists who like refinement might opt for old favorites such as percale for bed linen and damask for table linen, while lovers of all things tactile can indulge in tapestry, brocade, crewelwork, and bouclé, whose woven patterns gives their surfaces a richness that looks warm and inviting. All these fabrics are great for heavy curtains and pillows. For a touch of luxury there is velvet, crushed velvet, devoré, corduroy, chenille, and fake fur. Even a throw or small pillow made in any of these fabrics will add depth and opulence to the surroundings. Natural textures abound in raw silk, burlap, jute, wool, and felt – their innate irregularities give a mellow, down-to-earth, and fuss-free effect wherever they are used. If you want to turn back the clock, old-fashioned options include antique lace, embroidery, and quilts. Their time-worn textures and faded glamour are the perfect finishing touch in a bedroom.

● Color and texture give depth to an elaborate tapestry chair cover (above). The raw qualities of the natural fabrics in shades of brown and cream complement the earthy tones of the walls, fireplace, and leather chair (right). The sumptuous folds of the fabrics in this bedroom (overleaf) engender peace and relaxation.

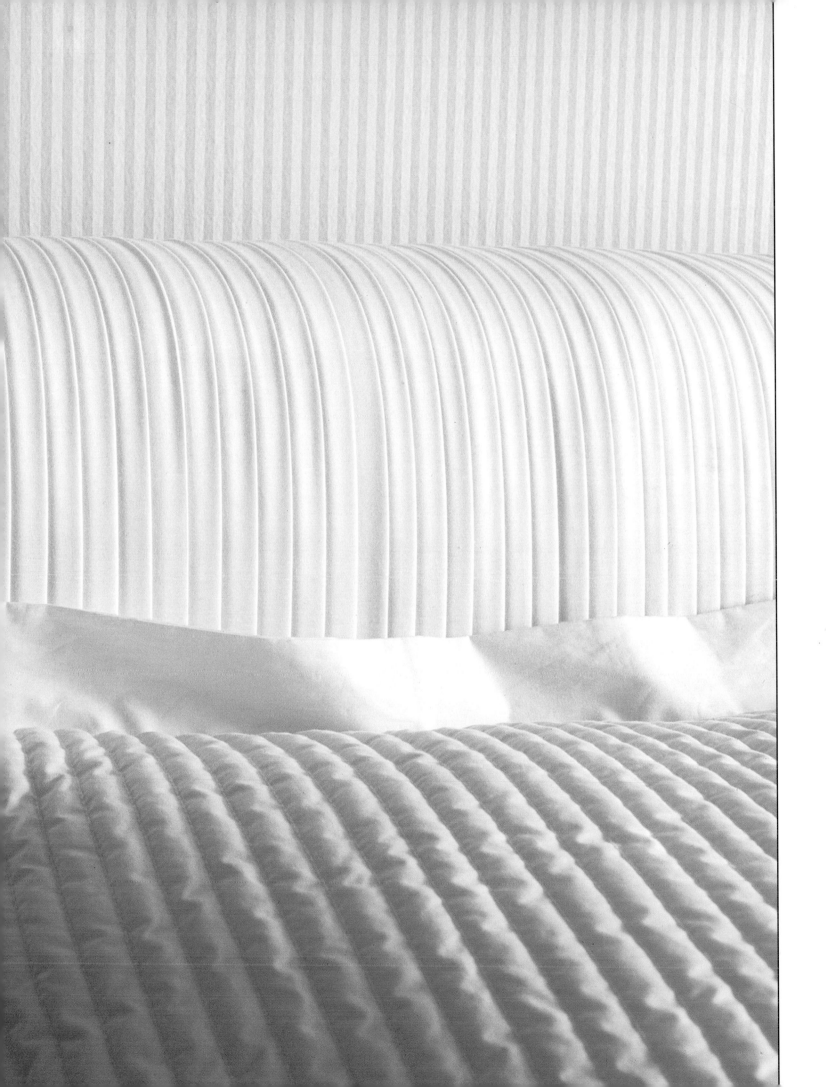

# textured flooring

Floors provide a large surface area on which to experiment with texture and indulge in the contrasts of different materials. For a coarse texture, choose natural materials such as sisal, coir, seagrass, and rush matting – especially those designs that have a knotty looped weave. Carpets that have similar textural qualities include cord and some of the more rugged wool carpets. It's also worth considering hard flooring such as old floorboards, rough-hewn flagstones, and brick, which all have wonderful natural irregularities.

For flooring with a smoother finish, you could lay linoleum, quarry tiles, parquet, marble, vinyl, ceramic and encaustic tiles, cork, or terrazzo. Carpets at the more expensive end of the market have a finer quality, too. Although a full-size Persian carpet or a floor covering made from linen or the softest wool may be beyond the price range of many people, a good compromise is to splurge on a rug made in these pricier materials and place it on polished wood or a rougher textured carpet for maximum impact. More economical still, yet just as good for introducing small areas of texture into a room, are modern kelims, dhurries, and rag rugs.

● As well as providing warmth underfoot, rugs allow you to play with a range of textures. Here, a cotton rug is placed on bare wood (right below) and an Oriental rug on a coir carpet (right above). The painted wooden floors (far right) make a stunning backdrop for the collection of blue-and-white throws and quilts.

# comfort
## corners

Set aside somewhere in your house and make it a special place devoted to relaxation and comfort. Retreat there at the end of a stressful day to drink a cup of herbal tea, think through a problem, make a decision, or simply enjoy the moment.

Choose a chair in the corner of a living room, study, or bedroom; a window seat on a landing; a rocking chair in a sunroom; a hammock in an attic; or some floor pillows in an alcove. The perfect spot might be near a fire, somewhere that is warmed by shafts of morning sunshine, one that looks out over an uplifting view, or one that faces an inspiring picture.

Give your chosen place a focal point – this could be the chair or pillow itself, a stunning fabric cover, a plant, or an adjacent window. Make sure the chair is as comfortable as possible, piled with pillows, and perhaps with a small footstool. Then surround yourself with things that make you feel good: favorite colors; a few treasured objects in a pleasing group; the soothing sounds of music; a refreshing scent from a bowl of potpourri or fresh flowers; soft lighting from a lamp or candles; or the beloved family pet.

● Abundant floral fabrics bring feminine style to a comfortable bedroom corner (opposite). Mirrors can be effectively positioned to give a fascinating series of views from an armchair (left). The perfect position for a contemplative corner is one that is bathed in plenty of sunlight (above).

*"When the voices of children are
heard on the green
And laughing is heard on the hill."*

WILLIAM BLAKE

# Sound

Mind, body, and spirit can all be altered by the
powerful force of sound. Humans can detect noises as
quiet as the rustling of autumn leaves or as loud as a jet
engine; as pleasant as early-morning birdsong or as
stressful as the constant rumble of traffic. So it is
imperative that noise pollution is banished from the
home and replaced by sounds that please and inspire.

Try opening a window and enjoying the repertoire
that nature has to offer. Some sounds, from flowing
water to a gentle breeze, are tranquil; others, such as a
crash of thunder or a downpour of rain, are powerful
or exhilarating. You could also introduce music to your
home to stir the emotions and evoke feelings of joy,
reverence, or serenity. Or you could create an especially
quiet room where, but for the sound of your own
breath, there is total silence. Use your sense of hearing
to heal and soothe you, and to transform your house
into a haven of calm.

● Nature offers a wealth of therapeutic sounds – from
the rustle of the wind in the trees to the crashing of
waves on the shore.

# houses
## by the sea

Childhood memories of vacations by the sea stay with you forever. The experience is so intense that years later you can still recall the tiniest details – the games you played, the rock pools you explored, and the house you stayed in.

Anyone who has ever rented a cottage at the coast for summer vacations will appreciate the unique pleasures of living by the sea. You can be bathed in intense light from the endless skies; you can breathe fresh, clean air and enjoy the smell and taste of the sea; you can be lulled to sleep by the hypnotic sound of the waves crashing on the shore and woken by the cries of seabirds. Bringing you so close to the elements, a beach retreat encourages you to sample a simpler and more natural way of life.

Inside the house, decoration, furniture, and fabrics are uncomplicated, unfussy, and unpretentious so that nothing detracts from the view of the dunes and the distant, watery horizon. White paint and a splash of blue complement the bright light that streams in through windows dressed in the sheerest of fabrics. Pieces of furniture are precious because they are familiar and comfortable, not because they

● Uncomplicated style is central to a house by the sea. White walls, splashes of nautical blue, simple fabrics, and comfortable, versatile furniture all create the perfect setting for relaxed living. When you throw open the doors, the dunes become your backyard and the beach your playground.

"My soul is full of longing for the
secret of the sea,
And the heart of the great ocean
Sends a thrilling pulse through me."

HENRY WADSWORTH LONGFELLOW

are priceless antiques. Sun-bleached wood, comfortable chairs, and well-worn sofas are the order of the day. Folding chairs and tables are a good idea so that meals can be enjoyed outdoors or in, depending on the weather.

Underfoot are wooden boards, rugs, and stray grains of sand. Furniture is strewn with throws that can double as picnic blankets, while fishermen's baskets make ideal hampers or log baskets. Fill shelves and line the walls with treasures from beachcombing expeditions; shells, floats, fronds of seaweed, pebbles, and pieces of driftwood jostle for position beside seascapes, model boats, and sketches drawn on lazy afternoons.

Even if your home is in the city, you can emulate simple beach style to bring a breath of fresh air and the sense of tranquility that is an integral part of life by the sea.

● Shells, starfish, floats, and fishing nets are the only adornment the house needs, making it feel at one with its seaside surroundings (opposite). Living so close to the elements gives life a special edge; a meal lit by lanterns seems all the more cozy as the storm rages outside (above).

# sound
## effects

The types of sound that surround you at home can have a significant impact on the quality of your life. Although there is little you can do about location – short of moving – you can take a number of positive steps to reduce the onslaught of competing sounds from both external and internal sources.

### Outside noise

The noise from cars, planes, road construction, and neighbors can shatter the peace of a home and be a source of stress. In general, heavy, thick materials such as concrete and stone are best for blocking out intrusive sounds, since they vibrate less than lighter ones such as wood and deaden the sound waves more effectively.

Certain structural changes, such as insulated walls, double doors and windows, false ceilings, floating floors, and special wall linings, will help to combat noise pollution in the home, especially from sounds transmitted by vibration through walls and floors – noisy plumbing or the hum of a next-door vacuum, for example. But if these structural elements haven't already been built into your home, and if it isn't practical to add them, you could look at other ways of minimizing the problem.

To protect yourself from sounds that travel through the air and in through doors and windows – this includes noise from traffic and aircraft, as well as nearby trains, factories, and machinery – install double-glazing, shutters, and double doors, along with other measures such as filling in any gaps and cracks. All these steps are valuable for heat conservation as well as for combating noise; thus your quieter home will also be cozier.

## Noises within

Echoes seem to ring around empty rooms because sound waves bounce off hard surfaces such as walls, ceilings, and floors. While a sparsely furnished room might be a useful way of creating an illusion of space, a large amount of reverberating noise in an almost empty room can be quite stressful, especially in high-traffic areas such as stairwells and halls, where the constant pounding of feet and echoing of footsteps can become a source of irritation.

Most people want to live in spaces that are cozy, quiet, and enclosed. This can be done by adding materials that absorb sound: try using lots of fabric – either as curtains at windows and doorways or to line the walls – plus carpets, rugs, and books. If you would like to set aside one quiet and peaceful place in the home, then a room full of books is ideal, since walls that are lined with bookshelves provide a natural barrier to sound.

Once you have banished all unwanted noise, you can fill your house with sounds you like, not ones that are imposed on you. You could set up a music system, perhaps with speakers in the bedroom, kitchen, and bathroom; indulge in new-age sounds, such as birdsong or whale music; install a small indoor fountain; or hang up some wind chimes or bells. As long as your chosen background noise makes you feel at peace, it will be a valuable addition to your home.

● The wall-to-wall carpet and soft accessories in this lofty staircase help to absorb noise from the impact and echo of footsteps.

| Wealth | Fame | Relationships |
|--------|------|---------------|
| Authority | Tai chi | Creativity |
| Contemplation | Career | Helpful people |

● Wind chimes, crystals, lamps, and flowers (this page and opposite) all attract beneficial chi and enhance the feng shui of your home. Use the chart called the bagua (above) to see how various areas of the house correspond to certain aspects of your life.

# feng shui

The Chinese art of placement, known as feng shui, is a way of ordering and arranging possessions to make sure the home is peaceful, healthy, happy, and prosperous. It has been practiced for thousands of years in the East, where it is so much a part of life that no building is designed without consulting a feng shui master.

Feng shui is all about maintaining a beneficial flow of life-giving energy – or chi – in a person's surroundings. Items that block, stagnate, or interfere with this energy, such as clutter, badly positioned furniture, sharp angles, or lifeless corners, should all be avoided, as they are thought to cause physical, spiritual, interpersonal, or financial problems among the people who live there. Once the energy is flowing again, however, all will be well.

The first action to take is to clear the house of all clutter. Be ruthless and pare down possessions to a minimum. Don't just put things into closets – hoarded junk, wherever it is, blocks chi and compromises your well-being.

To work out how to arrange what you keep, you'll need to draw up a template, or bagua (see left). Place it over a plan of your house, or a plan of just one room, orienting it so that the front door or the entrance to the room is at the bottom of the section called Career. You'll see that the bagua divides up your living space into nine sections, each of which represents a different aspect of your life. The possessions that fill these spaces affect the energy there and can be moved to bring about change.

The area in the top left-hand corner of the bagua represents Wealth, which has as much to do with personal blessings as it does with money. Next to it is Fame, which concerns inner clarity and inspiration. Relationships is the area concerned with your family and friends as well as your partner, while Authority is about your ancestors, your boss, and your parents. Creativity is associated with offspring and personal projects; Contemplation includes knowledge, spirituality, and

introspection; Career represents your path in life; and Helpful People refers to those with whom you enjoy mutual help and support. The central square is called Unity, or Tai chi, and is important for maintaining health and life – always keep this area of a building or a room still and uncluttered.

Sometimes a room or building, especially if it is L-shaped, lacks a whole section of the bagua, and this is considered bad feng shui. For example, if the area called Wealth is missing, it could explain why you have been experiencing financial problems; if Relationships is absent, the chances are that this aspect of your life is unfulfilled. There are, however, solutions: you can place a mirror so that it appears to extend the room in

a particular direction, or you can use a light or a wind chime to activate the missing part of the bagua – even if this means putting them outside in the backyard. These remedies rebalance the energy flow and allow you to experience good luck previously denied to you.

Bad feng shui can also be caused by the negative energy – known as cutting chi – that emanates from sharp edges or straight lines. For example, the corner of a piece of furniture is harmful if it points at you, as are the sharp angles from a neighbor's gabled roof if they are directed at your window. You should always try to soften or deflect cutting chi. Hide the edges of a square table under a piece of fabric, and overcome the problem of the roof next door by hanging a special mirror outside your house to reflect the damaging energy.

Once you have defended yourself against harmful influences, you can start to activate areas of the bagua to improve specific aspects of your life. This is achieved by placing objects in certain places to invite good fortune. You could use mirrors, lamps, wind chimes, plants, indoor fountains, crystals, fresh flowers, an aquarium, some bells, or a bamboo flute – all are most auspicious, some especially so in certain areas of the bagua. It is thought that placing a plant – particularly the Chinese money plant – in Wealth will work wonders with your finances, while a crystal in Relationships will improve your marriage prospects.

Often you need only make the most subtle alterations to your surroundings to achieve positive results. Give careful thought to what you need before you start, and don't try to do everything all at once – your motivation should not be greed or selfishness but a magnanimous desire to bring about change for the better.

● Round tables attract good feng shui because, unlike square or rectangular ones, there are no sharp edges to give off negative energy, or cutting chi. A mirror in the dining room is also auspicious as the reflection of food symbolizes abundance.

*"How hot the scent is
of the summer rose."*

ROBERT GRAVES

# Scent

Through the sense of smell, you can transport yourself to a different place, a different mood, or a different time. Aromas, more than any of the other sensual experiences, can trigger powerful associations. Consider harnessing those perceptions to make your surroundings more welcoming, relaxing, healing, refreshing, seductive, or nurturing – whatever seems right at the time.

Return to childhood with a drop of your mother's perfume. Comfort yourself by filling your kitchen with the smell of a baking cake. Re-create a lazy weekend in the country by opening a window and filling a vase with fresh flowers. Conjure up warm climes with aromatic herbs and spices. Transcend a chilly season with the smell of freshly mown grass. Bring back memories of cozy winters with cinnamon, pine needles, and an open fire. For a healthy, happy, and peaceful home, follow your nose.

● Flowers freshly picked from the backyard bring a delicate scent that relieves stress and lifts the spirits. Place sweet-smelling blooms in the warmth of a sunny window (opposite) or on a bedside table (left).

# looking at
# room scents

In an age when the air you breathe may be polluted by anything from vehicle exhaust and tobacco smoke to cleaning products and synthetic perfumes, you have to take steps to counter this by making your home a naturally scented oasis of peace and well-being. Before introducing any new scents, start by avoiding cleaning materials that contain strong chemicals and by banishing artificial air-freshening products. You can then begin to add some of the wonderfully fragrant things nature has to offer – flowers, spices, herbs, fragrant foods, and essential oils.

● Flowers, pinecones, herbs, spices – nature offers a wealth of enticing fragrances (this page). Scented candles in the perfume of your choice will help to create a relaxing and welcoming atmosphere. Add a few drops of an essential oil to a ceramic oil burner or mix with water in a mister for a therapeutic room scent. The aromas that emanate from the kitchen – freshly brewed coffee, warm crusty bread, wine, cheese, and an aromatic salad – all evoke a sense of comfort and well-being (opposite).

## Fresh air and perfumed plants

Simply opening a window is often the best way to improve the air quality in your home. To make the atmosphere more sensual, grow scented plants near the house. Such fragrant flowers as honeysuckle, old-fashioned roses, or sweet peas will reward you every time you open the door or brush past them. Plant window boxes with perfumed flowers, such as lily-of-the-valley, stock, nicotiana, and jasmine, or choose a selection of wonderfully aromatic herbs and place them on windowsills in every room. Then just throw open the window and enjoy their scent.

## Nature's harvest

Place baskets or ornamental bowls full of potpourri around the house. You can easily prepare your own blends by gathering flower petals, slices of citrus fruit, and special finds such as pinecones, leaves, berries, and seed heads. Dry them and sprinkle with essential oils, then add a little orrisroot. A suitable summer selection might include a mixture of rose petals and heads of lavender; a winter blend could combine herbs such as bay and rosemary, and spices such as cloves and cinnamon.

## Questions to consider when scenting your home

● Could you replace artificially scented room sprays and cleaning products with more natural alternatives?

● Do you prefer scents that are floral, spicy, herbal, woody, earthy, sweet, or musky?

● Which are your favorite scented flowers?

● Are you drawn to a particular essential oil?

● Which foods have the most mouth-watering aroma?

● Do certain scents fill you with a sense of happiness and well-being?

● Bring natural scents indoors with dishes of aromatic potpourri and dried flowers revived with essential oils.

## Burning desires

One of the most therapeutic ways to fragrance the home is to place a few drops of essential oil in a ceramic ring over a lamp, in a diffuser above a candle, or in an electric vaporizer. This will heighten your level of comfort, or, on expert advice, may be used to treat a specific health problem. Naturally scented candles offer a wonderful choice of perfumes, in addition to casting a gentle light.

## About the house

Revive age-old housekeeping practices by choosing traditional cleaning materials – beeswax polish fills the room with its inimitable aroma, and bicarbonate of soda or vinegar clean kitchen surfaces without leaving harmful chemical residues. Added to water, essential oils with antiseptic properties can be used as disinfectants: try tea-tree oil, pine, thyme, or lavender. Keep a nonaerosol mister filled with water and a few drops of essential oil to use as a room spray for freshening the home when needed.

## The good life

Brew up a pot of fresh coffee, bake a loaf of bread, set the lunch table with fragrantly dressed salads and farmhouse cheeses, and open a bottle of wine – all will fill the room with the sort of mouth-watering aromas that are an integral part of a sweet-smelling home. They make you feel content not just because you know they taste good but because you associate them with good times and with the sense of anticipation and celebration they evoke.

# using scents

There is a scent for every room in the house, so plan your perfumes as carefully as you would a color scheme.

The bathroom is perhaps the best place to indulge yourself: Soak away your stress or overcome fatigue by treating yourself to a scented bath. Add an essential oil recommended by an aromatherapist (some oils are not suitable during pregnancy or for certain medical conditions) or fill a sachet with specially selected herbs and flowers and infuse it in the bath water.

Take scents into the bedroom to give you a good night's rest. Herb pillows filled with lavender, chamomile, or marjoram will help you sleep soundly. Store clothes and linen in chests and boxes made of aromatic woods such as

sandalwood, cedar, or juniper; tuck in sprigs of woodruff, lavender sachets, rose petals, or sweet-smelling herbs in gauze pouches. Paper impregnated with geranium or citrus oils can be used to line drawers (take care not to stain your fabrics), and pomanders made from oranges studded with cloves will fill your closet with a deliciously spicy aroma – and keep the moths away.

Living rooms benefit from the comforting and distinctive smell of an open fire, which also helps to circulate air. Add a topnote to this therapeutic effect by throwing on some pinecones, aromatic herbs such as rosemary or sage, or fruit woods. Kitchens and dining rooms are naturally filled with a wealth of wonderful food smells. Enhance the homey aromas by harvesting bunches of fresh herbs and hanging them to dry in the kitchen. You can then enjoy their fragrance – as well as their taste – throughout the year.

● Plants with aromatic leaves can enhance a room's overall atmosphere and comfort (opposite). All the work is done for you in a kitchen filled with the mouth-watering smells of cooking and drying herbs (above). The addition of deliciously scented blooms stirs the senses in this hall (overleaf).

# flowers

Fresh flowers bring nature – with its calming influence, wonderful colors, and glorious scents – into your home. Freshly cut or growing in pots, gathered in armfuls from the backyard, or bought in bunches from a florist, flowers lift your spirits and brighten your surroundings, making town and country dweller alike feel more in touch with the natural world.

Flower arrangements don't have to be large or costly to make an impression. Some overblown roses in a teacup, a single tulip in an elegant vase, or a jelly jar filled with cow parsley or willow herb all capture the spirit of your garden and the beauty of nature, and can be more appealing than a formal display. A dinner table, breakfast tray, bedside table, or hallway should never be without flowers.

If you have a yard, consider devoting part of it to growing a constant supply of flowers for cutting. The pleasure they give will make it well worth the effort. Harvest blooms in the morning or evening and display them in as many interesting containers as your imagination will allow.

By growing bulbs in pots, you can also enjoy flowers in the winter months – hyacinths are a favorite for their sweet fragrance, daffodils for their cheerful color. When it's too cold to spend any length of time outdoors, venture out just long enough to gather berries and evergreen foliage to display indoors, and to cut a few stems from budding shrubs such as heliotrope, witch hazel, and wintersweet. Place in water and the warmth of the house will encourage the buds to open, inspiring thoughts of warmer months.

Flowering potted plants are also cheering, and some will even purify the air in your house. Gerberas, moth orchids, tulips, cyclamen, Christmas cacti, chrysanthemums, and peace lilies are all thought to remove harmful chemicals from the atmosphere, so are doubly valuable to maintaining a peaceful home.

● Delicate pink-flushed hydrangeas in a simple cream-colored pot provide an informal display (left). A stately bouquet of white lilies in a glass vase adds a touch of sophistication to this dining room (opposite).

● Essential oil from aromatic plants such as eucalyptus (top left) makes a natural room scent. Wooden balls impregnated with fragrant oils (top right) will perfume drawers and closets, while a ceramic oil burner will fill the room with a therapeutic aroma (above). Store essential oils in a glass bottle (left).

# aromatherapy
## for the home

Essential oils, extracted from aromatic plants, make wonderfully therapeutic room scents. A ceramic oil burner is a good investment, allowing you to experiment with a variety of fragrances in different rooms for various purposes. The burner will have space for a votive light, above which is a small dish into which you pour some water and a few drops of an essential oil. The heat of the candle warms the water, vaporizing the oil and releasing its magical scent. Alternatively, electric diffusers perform the same function without a flame, or you could place some oil into a special light-bulb diffuser – an earthenware ring that fits over the bulb of a table lamp, heating up to activate the oil.

Some essential oils have particular healing properties, while others will give a general lift or create a feeling of relaxation. These oils can be very potent, so it's best to consult an aromatherapist before you begin. Then you can fill your rooms with either one single scent that is a clear personal favorite or a specially prescribed blend.

Aromatherapy oils can be divided into families. Some, such as the citrus oils, need little introduction – orange, lemon, lime, and grapefruit are clean and refreshing. Floral oils, such as geranium, rose, neroli, lavender, or ylang ylang, have a heady perfume, while herbal options include marjoram, peppermint, and rosemary. For a clean medicinal aroma, choose one of the camphoraceous oils, such as eucalyptus and tea tree, as well as camphor itself. Rich, spicy scents are obtained from ginger and coriander, woody or outdoorsy fragrances from cedarwood, sandalwood, and juniper.

Oils from within the same group can be combined to make harmonious blends, but certain groups have a natural affinity for one another: florals mix well with citrus or woody scents, and spices and citrus oils make good partners, too. Some oils are classic stress relievers, so if you are feeling tense, try lavender, ylang ylang, or chamomile. Others, such as rosemary, orange, and eucalyptus, are good for reviving you after a tiring day.

"*Strange to see how a good dinner and feasting reconciles everybody.*"

SAMUEL PEPYS

# taste

Enticing tastes can be as simple as a cup of tea and a slice of freshly baked cake or as complex as the menu of a special dinner party. Food brings people together to share one another's company and to savor and celebrate the wonderful variety and intensity of flavors available. Sun-ripened fruit, luscious chocolate, tender spring vegetables, exotic spices, comforting grains and pasta – all are truly delicious as well as sustaining.

Your kitchen should be devoted to the enjoyment of food. To make it as convivial as possible, fill it with mouthwatering aromas, sensational flavors, and visual feasts. When you return from the store, instead of putting food out of sight in cupboards, put it on display and enjoy anticipating the tastes to come: pile fresh, fragrant tomatoes in an earthenware dish; place bright, shiny lemons in a glass bowl; fill a rustic basket with crisp green apples. Such tantalizing sights will become an integral part of the decoration of your home – a sign that food is the way to the heart.

● Flavored with fresh herbs, bottles of homemade oils and vinegars bring the essence of summer to your table all year round.

# kitchens

A primitive desire to be warmed and nourished makes people gravitate toward the kitchen, its open fire or stove providing the perfect surroundings in which to relax and enjoy good food and pleasant company. Today's kitchen is no longer the domain of the cook, but is an all-embracing, welcoming, and informal room used for chatting, entertaining, and working as well as cooking, eating, and washing. It is the hub of the peaceful home.

Many people feel most comfortable in a traditional country kitchen whose unstructured style will adapt to the changing demands of the family over the years. Others love kitchens that are driven by simple, modern style and have a uniform, streamlined look that re-creates the lines of a professional kitchen.

Whatever mood you wish to create, everything must run smoothly and be planned for calm efficiency rather than frantic chaos. The room should be laid out so you don't have to walk a long way to put away the dishes when you've washed them, for example, and so you have somewhere to put hot pans when you remove them from the burner.

Then there's the question of how to incorporate appliances such as dishwashers, washing machines, and microwaves into a room that might need a softer and less industrial image to be restful. To prevent the machines from taking over, either conceal them in cabinets or behind decorative panels, or, if space in your home permits, consider housing them in a separate room altogether. Alternatively, you could liberate yourself totally by trying to live without them – you might be surprised at how rewarding such a simple approach can be.

A kitchen will automatically feel less utilitarian and more welcoming if it contains at least one piece of freestanding furniture: a table, a hutch, an armoire, an armchair, a bench, or even a sofa will all sit happily alongside built-in units if you have them.

● When planning a large kitchen that is used for many different activities, it is helpful to divide up the space into several zones, each with its own function. Here, special areas are set aside for eating, food preparation, and storage, giving the room a coherent look as well as making an efficient workspace.

## The Peaceful Home

● Storage and display are interchangeable in traditional kitchens, as jars, pans, pitchers, and plates are too attractive to be confined to a cupboard. Arranged on windowsills, lining shelves, or hanging from hooks, treasured items add life and character (right above and below). The heart of a farmhouse kitchen is its homey cooking range, which provides warmth, nourishment, and the perfect place to dry linen (far right). Whatever type of stove you have, make it the focal point of the kitchen.

If you think you'd miss the storage space provided by a built-in kitchen, try some time-honored alternatives for creative display: hang saucepans from a batterie de cuisine; suspend utensils from a Shaker-style peg rack; or stack dishes on a wooden plate rack. Other additions might include some stoneware jars, a meat safe, old enamel tins, an egg basket, a butcher's block, or a ceramic sink.

If your kitchen feels right, works well, and is filled with the good things in life, it doesn't matter what size it is or how little it cost. From the moment you make that first cup of coffee in the morning to the time you prepare a bedtime mug of cocoa, you will be able to enjoy a room that is easygoing and uncomplicated.

● Traditional kitchens have a wonderful air of informality. A long pine table, a side table, a metal storage rack, and a small armchair add to this room's comfort and sense of style (left), while a collection of copperware hangs on the walls and fireplace as a decorative solution to the lack of cabinet space (above).

# dining rooms

In the age of fast food, when snacking and grazing are the norm, it's healthy to set aside a place in the house that is devoted to eating and appreciating wholesome, home-cooked food in relaxed surroundings. If you don't have a separate dining room, make part of the living room or kitchen into an eating area. Whether you have a romantically decorated dining room complete with buffet and candelabra or a scrubbed pine kitchen table surrounded by tavern chairs, your aim should be to make it genial and cheerful.

A formal dining room that is not used very often can easily become a stuffy and unlived-in part of the house. Instead of closing the door until your next dinner party, use it for everyday meals and as an additional quiet workplace for letter-writing or reading. Decorate it in warm, dark colors to contrast with white china and linen if it is the setting for dramatic evening occasions, or opt for lighter and brighter shades if it is more often used for informal meals and family suppers.

Folding or drop-leaf tables, or even simple trestles, are ideal, as they can be used for an intimate meal for two or extended to accommodate a number of guests. Seating should be as comfortable as possible, so add pillows and covers, and choose dining chairs with gently sloping rather than upright backs – those with arms provide maximum comfort. Stylish table settings that make the most of linen, china, glass, flatware, candles, and flowers will add to the sense of occasion.

● This dining room and adjoining living room are decorated in a similar style to give a sense of continuity (top left). The linen chair covers and tablecloth create an air of restrained formality. Simplicity is the key to this serene scheme (top right), where metal chairs, topiary, and the open door invite garden-style dining indoors. Dining rooms should look as good by day as they do by night – this one is flooded with sun at lunchtime and then filled with candlelight for dinner (bottom left). A pine hutch and rush-seated chairs create the perfect farmhouse setting (bottom right).

# looking at table settings

Like the scenery in a theater, table settings can conjure up different situations, moods, or styles. You can introduce different props – table linen, china, flatware, flowers, and candles – changing them to create special effects and to suit any occasion. From classic combinations to idiosyncratic improvisations, it's great fun to experiment and add personal expression to mealtimes.

## Theme and variations

The most inventive table settings are themed, however subtly, using a particular color scheme, a seasonal flower, or a certain image as a recurring motif. A summer lunch could feature roses massed in a central table decoration, single blooms at each place setting, and floral fabric for tablecloth and napkins. For a Valentine's meal, you could have heart-shaped place cards, red ribbons to tie together bundles of flatware, and heart-shaped chocolates.

## Table linen

This forms the backdrop to the drama. A crisp white cloth is the perfect foil for delicate porcelain – either plain or patterned – and the finest glass. Ethnic prints go well with chunky, rustic tableware, and gingham is the perfect partner for brightly colored dishes.

Antique table linen has timeless charm, especially when layered with lace for a delicate look. To cover a large table with something slightly less precious, buy a length of solid material and dye it or decorate it with fabric paints, or stitch on a contrasting border. Alternatively, buy several yards of inexpensive cotton and drape it around the table in opulent swags. Circular tables, especially, cry out for floor-length cloths, perhaps overlaid with smaller square ones in different fabrics that build up a richly layered look. Napkins can be chosen to match the tablecloth or to contrast with

● Choose china, flatware, and glassware that reflect your tastes and are appropriate for the occasion (this page and opposite).

## Classic combinations

● White damask, fine porcelain, crystal glassware, silver flatware, roses

● Provençal fabric, French country china, colored glassware, sunflowers

● Antique lace, floral bone china, handblown glass, silverware, sweet peas

● Gingham, café-style china, chunky glass tumblers, stainless-steel flatware, tulips

it. Either enclose each one in a napkin ring or tie it decoratively according to the theme of your party – use raffia, string, or ribbon, perhaps with a leaf or a flower tucked underneath the bow to make a pretty display.

## Dishes, glass, and flatware

To heighten the sense of anticipation, the table should be laden with attractive plates, bowls, glassware, and flatware. For formal dining, use decorative underplates at each place setting, and surround them with rows of flatware and clusters of glasses. Each piece should be polished and sparkling for maximum effect.

For restrained elegance, choose the finest bone china or porcelain, crystal glassware, and antique silver. For farmhouse style, use stoneware pottery, handblown glass, and simple flatware. For a bright, modern look, opt for colorful china and plastic. For the perfect afternoon tea, hunt for cups and saucers in flea markets and team them with accessories such as a cake stand, a lidded sugar bowl, and cake forks. Your dishes, glasses, and flatware don't have to match – in fact, an assortment of pieces collected over the years lends a special character that is sometimes lacking when everything is perfectly coordinated.

## Flowers and finishing touches

Choose flowers in spring and summer, richly colored leaves in the fall, and berries and evergreen foliage in winter. These can be made into one generous and striking arrangement in the center of the table, or individual ones for each place setting. Centerpieces can also be made by filling a large bowl with green apples or citrus fruit – en masse, they have tremendous impact and provide a wonderful splash of color.

Don't forget to add candles – branched candelabra or a number of single candlesticks for dinner parties, an assortment of different containers for less formal events. If you are expecting a number of guests, create a seating plan and make special place cards. You could go to town with colored paper and inks, or even use luggage labels and tie them to the backs of the chairs.

● A dramatic and sultry dining table is created by combining shades of gold, black, and red in richly patterned china, deep-colored fabric napkins, crimson blooms, a copper vase, and softly glowing lighting.

# entertaining

From a simple supper for a few close friends to a large and extravagant birthday party, one of the best ways to mark a special occasion or show affection for those you love is to invite them into your peaceful home to share good food and convivial company. Entertaining should be a relaxed and generous affair, not fraught with social airs and graces, so make your home as welcoming as possible to capture that special party spirit, and let the fun begin.

For an evening gathering, line the driveway with lights and drape strings of Christmas-tree lights in trees, shrubs, and around the front door to guide the guests when they arrive. For parties that celebrate a birthday or a festive occasion such as Thanksgiving, Christmas, or Easter, set the mood from the moment everyone enters the house by adorning the front door and the hallway with flowers, foliage, and seasonal decorations. Wreaths, garlands, and baskets all look striking.

Inside the house, the table should be the focus of the dining area. Whether in daylight or at night, it should sparkle with candles, polished glasses, and gleaming china. Choose a menu that takes advantage of fresh seasonal produce and serve the dishes in grand style on platters and in generous bowls, each one presented with care and flair. Successive courses should be

● This high-ceilinged room is perfect for entertaining with a touch of grandeur. Natural light mixes with candlelight, which is reflected in mirrors and the crystal chandelier, while comfortable chairs are gathered around a table set with elegant china, glasses, and flowers.

served at a leisurely pace, allowing guests time to relax and savor the occasion. It is wonderful to round the meal off with an indulgent dessert, followed by fine coffee and chocolates. When the evening is over, revive a childhood tradition by presenting small gifts to your guests as they depart.

Relaxed, cozy, and intimate suppers for friends – whether eaten in the warmth of the kitchen, on TV tables around the living-room fire or in a sunroom or porch – may be more casual but are just as rewarding. Forget all things lavish and luxurious – for this type of gathering anything goes. Let the food and the conversation work their magic.

● To reflect the simple surroundings (above), a table is set with a plain white cloth and laden with delicious, home-cooked food. Get the day off to a fine start with breakfast served in a sunny nook (right), followed by an alfresco lunch on the deck (overleaf).

# dining
## alfresco

Eating outdoors is one of life's great pleasures. It gives you a breath of fresh air, makes you feel connected to the natural world, and allows you to spend quality time enjoying the scents, sounds, and sights of the garden, as well as the meal itself. If you live by the ocean or in the country, you'll find this an especially peaceful way to while away summer days.

Take your cue from the leisured Mediterranean way of life, where family and friends enjoy meals on a terrace or balcony in the warmer months. At breakfast, they enjoy the first gentle rays of sun, at lunch they sit in the shade of a tree or a canopy of vines, and in the cool evening air they watch the sun set as they talk and eat far into the night.

You don't have to have a large yard or spacious terrace – a small paved area by the back door that can accommodate a pretty folding table and chairs is all you need to experience the deep feeling of well-being that alfresco living can bring.

● A dining table, set for an informal lunch, is perfectly positioned next to the pool (top left). A canvas canopy on wooden supports makes an outdoor dining area from a narrow section of terrace (top right). Comfortable seating is provided by porch chairs that are brought outside and placed around a sturdy, weatherproof wooden table (bottom left). Afternoon tea is perfect under the shade of a simple outdoor umbrella (bottom right).

# PART THREE

# The Basics

In the words of the celebrated French architect Le Corbusier, "the house is a machine for living in." Well-designed buildings should be human-friendly places on an accessible scale, where everything functions efficiently, space is used creatively, shapes and lines are simple, and ergonomics are sound. These buildings are places that are in tune with the people who live in them, where beauty adapts to function, and where there is no conflict because human needs are met.

Getting the basic elements of your home environment right – its structure, windows, doors, floors, furniture, heating, and storage space – means that all parts of this machine run smoothly.

● The rustic character of this country dining room is
created by the wooden siding, simple window, plain
curtains, and hand-crafted furniture.

The reward for attending to these practicalities will be an untroubled lifestyle in which domestic tasks are not stressful chores but part of an easy and ongoing maintenance plan.

Begin by assessing where improvements can be made. Would your living room be cozier if you opened up that fireplace? Would terra-cotta tiles be more practical than carpet in your hall? Would a ceiling fan make a bedroom less stifling, or would a radiator make a difference on very cold days? Would an extra filing cabinet resolve your study's storage problems? Would additional electrical sockets make the kitchen easier to work in?

It can take time for your home to evolve in the way you want it to, for the basics to fit into place and for you to adapt to what's new. While you are finding your comfort level, remember that there are solutions to everything, that there is something to suit everyone, and that spending a lot of money is not always the answer.

Thoughtful and ingenious planning can save you time and expense, so don't be in too much of a rush to complete the task at hand. For example, rather than going for a "quick fix" and buying a new carpet, consider stripping the floorboards. Try hunting through antiques stores and thrift shops in search of an inexpensive armoire as an alternative to installing expensive built-in cupboards. And why not change the hardware, the doors, or simply the paint finish on your kitchen cabinets instead of replacing them altogether? If you have thought long and hard about what you need and how to achieve it, the end result will be of more value – not because it was the best that money could buy, but because it does the job perfectly.

If your house feels right, is well organized, and designed for practicality and efficiency, it will generate no anxiety, leaving you free to devote time and energy to things that really matter – including relaxation. Just imagine how much better life would be that way!

● A load-bearing wall exposed during building work is left unplastered – proving that getting back to basics can have striking results.

# windows and doors

Doors and windows make the exterior of a house – and the rooms inside – look welcoming and inviting. They add character in the same way that a person's eyes light up his or her face.

If you have an older home with all its original doors and windows, you are fortunate. In addition to a sense of history, they give the building a harmonious architectural style. So preserve these fixtures wherever you can, and don't be tempted to modernize an old house by removing paneled doors or installing metal window frames. If you have a new house, keep the modern windows and flush doors that were designed for it – they are just as appropriate as mullions and solid wood doors are for a country cottage.

If you have recently moved into an older property that no longer has its original doors and windows, scour flea markets or country auctions for replacements, or ask a carpenter to reproduce authentic designs. Check that newly bought or existing doors fit properly, have a smooth mechanism, prevent drafts, and do not rattle. Windows, too, should open and close easily. Your interior doors might be hollow modern ones with a flush finish, older-style paneled doors, or rustic ones made from planks. Glass doors can breathe new life into a dark room, while folding doors save space when opened and French doors make the most of an outdoor view. Door hardware should match the style of the house – an old plank door cries out for iron hinges and latches, while an elegant paneled door could have brass, china, or glass knobs and finger plates.

Similarly, certain windows suit certain situations – casements are perfect for country houses, sashes for town houses, dormers for attics, skylights for modern homes, and bays for traditional living rooms. The type of glass you use will alter the overall effect – try etched glass for privacy, leaded panes to cast soft shadows, or stained glass to flood the room with colored light. If you want the advantages of double-glazing, new units can usually be installed into an existing window, giving you the best of both worlds.

● First impressions count, so an original front door painted in harmonious colors makes a grand entrance (left). Small sash windows in a cottage kitchen (above) are too attractive to obscure with a curtain. Staining or painting a window frame in a dark color leads the eye to the view outside (opposite).

● Leaving internal doors open promotes a welcoming atmosphere, inviting you into successive rooms (far left). Shutters provide extra privacy at this bathroom window (left). Bold, bright paint colors make a feature of interesting paneled doors (far left and below).

# flooring

Choosing new flooring is an exciting opportunity to give a room a different image. Color, texture, and pattern will all be deciding factors, but practicality should also be high on your list of priorities.

Durability is the first consideration. Hard flooring materials such as wood, stone, ceramic tiles, linoleum, and vinyl wear well in high-traffic areas, as do some carpets – look for one that is densely woven and has a short pile, and ask the supplier for specific advice on its suitability. Imagine what several years of wear and tear will look like – some materials such as solid wood and stone, for example, age gracefully and become even more attractive with age. If you are choosing natural flooring, you'll find that sisal and coir are more resilient than jute and rush matting.

The next thing to consider is upkeep. However beautiful it looked in the showroom, a black-and-white tiled hall floor that shows every footprint and needs cleaning twice a day could be a stressful addition to your home. Kitchen floors get the most punishing treatment of all and need to be stain-resistant. Seek professional advice about sealing flagstones, wood, and ceramic tiles.

Comfort is another important factor, so look at a floor's heat- and sound-insulating properties and at its softness and warmth underfoot. Unless you have underfloor heating, stone or ceramic tiles can be cold, and wood can be noisy, especially for people in the rooms below.

Think about versatility, too. You can avoid being tied to a particular color scheme by choosing flooring in neutral colors. All the natural options – wood, stone, sisal, coir, jute, and cork – will adapt to any decorative changes you might want to make in the future.

● Glossy polished wood needs careful maintenance but gives a wonderfully rich finish to a spacious entrance hall (previous pages). Stone and chiseled slate combine to create a soft and practical time-worn look (right top), while an assortment of ceramic tiles are a colorful option in a bathroom (right bottom). The witty Kaffe Fassett bathmat complements the tiles beautifully and prevents the floor from becoming wet and slippery. The floor of a mud room has plain and patterned cement tiles that are durable and easy to clean (far right).

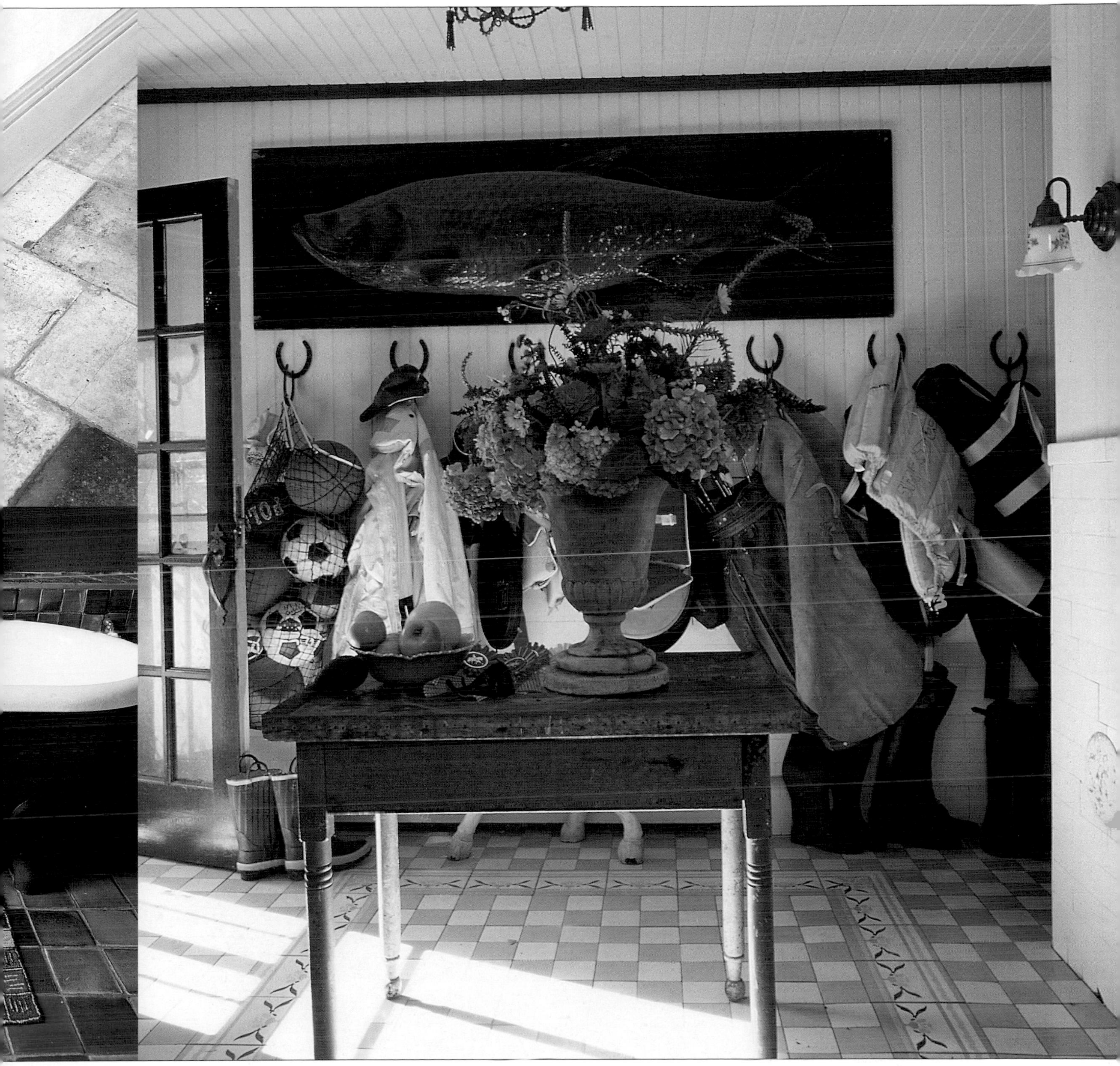

● Wooden floors improve with age, any tiny imperfections adding character to their naturally varied surface texture and color. They are also warm underfoot, which means they are perfect for a bedroom (opposite), while their forgiving nature makes them easy to live with in a living room (above right and left).

Environmental issues should also be taken into account, especially when choosing a wooden floor. Ideally, use reclaimed lumber – otherwise, avoid tropical hardwoods and buy only from guaranteed sustainable resources. Other "green" options include cork and linoleum.

Cost is always a deciding factor – both for the floor covering itself and for any expert help you may need to install it. But bear in mind that flooring is a major element in any room as well as a long-term investment, so it's wise to buy the best you can afford. Something handsome and long-lasting will look better and give you greater pleasure in years to come.

# versatile furniture

Our lives can be busy and unpredictable, so every piece of furniture in the house must earn its keep. Anything that serves more than one purpose and anything movable are worth their weight in gold.

Built-in kitchens, bathroom units, and bedroom closets are an extremely convenient way to utilize space – they are perfect for organizing lots of possessions without wasting an inch. But when it's time to move you have to leave them all behind – and face your original storage dilemmas all over again.

Instead, you might decide that it is better to opt for some freestanding pieces that will be more versatile and adaptable. Even if you aren't planning to move in the near future, you will have the freedom to redesign your rooms at any time – when you spring clean, when guests come to stay, or when you have a change of heart about the best position for a piece of furniture.

Take this idea to the limit and buy furniture on wheels for the ultimate movable feast. A butcher's block can be wheeled around the kitchen to provide extra counter space and an occasional table on casters will find many uses in the living room.

If space is at a premium, convertible sofas are a great asset, as are dining tables that can double as desks, freestanding bookshelves that act as room dividers, and blanket chests that can be used as impromptu benches.

● A pine drawer unit with an inset sink (right) is a brilliant alternative to a modern bathroom unit. Traditional hutches provide plenty of storage space in the kitchen, reducing the need for built-in cabinets and giving a more informal country look (far right).

## Storage ideas for every room

### Children's rooms
Plastic crates,
under-bed drawers

### Bedrooms
Armoires, built-in shelves

### Kitchens
Baskets, butcher's hooks,
baker's racks

### Bathrooms
Wheeled carts, wire shelf units

### Home offices
Bulletin boards, rattan in-trays

### Living rooms
Antique display cabinets,
alcove shelving

● A room divider made from a row of built-in
cupboards with central folding doors
separates the bathroom from the master
bedroom (top). A specially made cupboard-
and-drawer unit compensates for storage
space lost due to an attic conversion (right),
and a built-in closet makes the most of
an awkwardly shaped corner under the
eaves (far right).

# storage

Whether you fill your rooms to bursting with treasured objects or prefer an empty, minimalist look, you still need somewhere to keep the ironing board, the dishes, and the cleaning materials. If these things are always visible, they will spoil the harmony of your peaceful home.

It's easy to underestimate how many possessions you already have and how many you will accumulate in the future, so when planning your storage space double the amount you originally thought would be enough.

Next, be ruthless and discard the things you no longer like or never use – devotees of feng shui will know how important this is to their general well-being as well as to the overall look of the house. Divide the things you want to keep into three categories: one for things you rarely use, another for things you need from time to time, and the last for essentials. The first group can be relegated to the attic or basement. To house the second, which should be closer at hand, put shelving, cupboards, drawers, or boxes in halls, landings, corridors, alcoves, under beds, and in the area under the stairs – no corner should be wasted. It doesn't matter if it is stored at an awkwardly high or low level, since you won't need access to these items every day. Your third group, the essentials, can then be kept wherever they are needed most – on kitchen shelves, in bathroom cabinets, in chests of drawers in the bedroom, or in attractive boxes or baskets around the house.

When you have finished, every room will look more attractive and less cluttered. You won't have to sift frantically through piles of possessions every time you need something, things will no longer seem to vanish without a trace, and everything will have a proper place. You'll wonder how you ever managed before.

# surfaces

Worktops, tables, and desks throughout the house get more than their fair share of wear and tear, and you'll probably spend many hours using them for everything from preparing food and eating meals to working or reading the newspaper. They need to be well suited to the tasks you use them for.

The height of kitchen cabinets is critical to avoiding backache and neck strain. Standard kitchen cabinets are 3 feet high, but you may prefer to pay a little more to have tailor-made ones crafted to suit your height. Certain tasks may also require special arrangements – kneading dough requires a lower surface than chopping vegetables, for example, so incorporate a range of different options if you can. Desks need careful and individual attention, too – a comfortable height is usually around 2½ feet, though if you use a computer, the keyboard should be at lap level.

Kitchen worktops have to withstand a variety of factors – heat, dirt, moisture, fat, knives, stains, and strong acids and alkalies. Consider ceramic tiles for their sturdiness, though be aware that grouting can become discolored. Choose wood for its looks, which hold up even after years of use. Laminates and other man-made materials are easy to clean and difficult to damage, but they can seem clinical. Steel gives a professional image but it does need frequent cleaning to maintain its sparkle and it scratches easily. Granite and marble look wonderful, but are expensive (it's worth knowing that granite is more hard-wearing than marble, which must be protected by professional sealing).

● In this English farmhouse, pattern adorns all kinds of surfaces – including this wonderful tabletop (left). A charming old pine table (above) fulfills both a functional and aesthetic role.

● Replacing a gable end with an expanse of glass, and removing the ceiling to add height, creates a wonderfully light-filled living area (right). Exposed beams conjure up country-cottage style (above).

# structural features

It can be fascinating to see the skeleton of a house – its beams, plumbing, plaster, rafters, bricks, floorboards, or stone floors. These structural features are sometimes uncovered during construction work, sometimes added to during a conversion. Leaving them on display reveals a great deal about how the building was constructed as well as conveying a down-to-earth approach to your surroundings. Enlist the help of an architect or engineer to uncover your home's hidden potential.

Old buildings are the domain of exposed beams and bare stone walls, although attic conversions in newer properties can result in a modern take on this style. You might decide to leave rafters, strut supports, chimneys, and unplastered bricks on view rather than disguising them behind panels and wallboard. If you are adding a staircase leading to the attic, consider one with exposed treads and risers.

Knocking through ground-floor rooms to make an open-plan living area can reveal visible weight-bearing supports, which can become showcase features such as columns and archways. For the ultimate simplicity, recent building work might also allow you to leave bare plaster on the walls. In bathrooms or kitchens, consider using chrome-plated or polished brass pipes for sinks, bathtubs, and showers and leave them on show like your home's other bare bones.

# heating
## and cooling

Even though the human body can survive surprisingly varied extremes of temperature, it is only truly comfortable within a fairly narrow range. Your home should shield you from excessive changes in climate, warming or cooling you so you are at ease whatever the weather outside may be.

In general, the house needs to be warm enough for comfort, cool enough to avoid stuffiness. The warmth should be evenly distributed at all heights; there should be some air movement to stop a room from feeling stuffy; and there should be enough – but not too much – humidity. It's a fine balance to strike, especially as energy should be used responsibly, via efficient and well-insulated heating and cooking systems. The best way to preserve the earth's resources would be to build houses that make use of the lay of the land – for example, where hills or trees provide shelter from a prevailing wind, where vegetation shades the house from the searing sun, or even underground, where you could escape intense heat or cold.

A rather less radical solution for heating the home is to install up-to-date natural gas, electric or oil heating systems – after getting advice from a professional. Thermostatically controlled radiators, underfloor electrical elements and hot water pipes, or warm air emitted from ducts and grills all help maintain constant and comfortable temperatures. Other options include individual heat sources, such as up-to-date (and safe) heaters, wood-burning stoves, and, of course, the old-fashioned open fire with all its associations of companionship and warmth. If

● Scandinavian interiors were traditionally heated by wood-fired stoves clad with beautiful tiles (previous pages). Another good-looking favorite is the log fire, which adds character to a room even if it is not the principal source of heat (opposite). If modern radiators don't fit easily into the style of your home, they can be concealed behind decorative covers (left top and bottom).

you want to leave the ordinary modern radiators your
home has at present, you could hide them behind custom-
made covers or install classic period models or inspiring
contemporary designs.

When it's hot outside, air-conditioning is an effective
way to ensure that your home remains at a constant
temperature – a lifesaver on blistering summer days.
Ceiling and window fans also help to promote air
movement, while shutters and blinds can shade you from
the sun's rays and introduce a hint of tropical glamor.

● Easy ways to combat excessive heat include
ceiling fans (below) and an entire wall of windows
that slide and swing open (opposite).

● Clockwise from top left: Flowers bring life and warmth to areas of the house that are decorated in neutral colors. Fresh blooms are perfect for entrance hallways. An eclectic collection personalizes a living space, as does hand-painted detail on an antique headboard. A beautiful paisley-inspired stencil is used to decorate floorboards, while wallpaper covers a light switch to create an uninterrupted line.

# details

Look carefully at a peaceful room and the thoughtful, creative details will catch your eye. It is these little things, the finishing touches, that stamp your mark on your home and bring it to life. The way you decorate a windowsill or a mantelpiece with an impromptu display speaks volumes about your mood and style. The pretty paint effect that might have been time-consuming to achieve or the neat curtain treatment that complements the room to perfection will show what loving care has gone into this decorative scheme. An arrangement of fresh flowers, bringing nature and the seasons indoors, is a manifestation of the same creativity and care. Gleaming brass doorknobs and polished wooden floors are a mark of your dedication to maintaining a pleasant environment. All these details may be small, but they have a huge part to play because they turn wherever you live into a home.

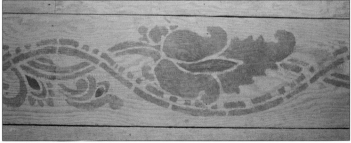

● Restraint is the key to elegant finishing touches around the home. A brass tieback gathers the curtain into soft, undulating folds and allows light to flood in through the window (left). Decorative details look equally striking in unexpected places. Small clusters of dried flowerheads make a pretty addition to a decorative display (above top), and a subtle, hand-stenciled border (above bottom) brings pattern to plain floorboards.

# resources

ABC Carpet & Home
888 Broadway
New York, NY 10003
(212) 473-3000, ext. 348

Baldwin Hardware Corporation
(800) 566-1986

Ballek's Garden Center
(800) 873-8878

Calico Corners (fabrics)
(800) 213-6366

Colonial Williamsburg
(furniture)
(800) 446-9240

Constance Greer Antiques
Amherst, NH 03031
(603) 673-5717

Country Floors
15 East 16th Street
New York, NY 10003
(212) 627-8300

Crossville Ceramics
P.O. Box 1168
Crossville, TN 38557
(615) 484-2110

Crown City Hardware
(800) 950-1047

Design Ideas
(800) 426-6396

Dione Antiques
(800) 487-0741

Du Pont Comfort Products
(800) 54-SLEEP

Dutch Boy Paints
(800) 828-5669

Eddie Bauer Home
(800) 426-8020 or (800) 645-7467

Harrington Brass Works Ltd., Inc.
7 Pearl Court, Allendale, NJ 07401
(201) 818-1300

Hunter Fan Company
2500 Frisco Avenue
Memphis, TN 38114
(901) 745-9222

IKEA (furniture)
(516) 681-4532 or (908) 289-4488

Janovic Plaza (paints and blinds)
(212) 982-6600

Karastan (carpets)
(800) 234-1120

Kirsch (window treatments)
(800) 528-1407

Laura Ashley (fabrics)
(800) 429-7678

Liz at Home by Liz Claiborne
(800) 527-7522

Maine Cottage Furniture Inc.
P.O. Box 935
Yarmouth, ME 04096
(207) 846-1430

Marvin Windows and Doors
(800) 346-5128

Old World Pewter
(800) 7-PEWTER

Pierre Deux (French furnishings)
870 Madison Avenue
New York, NY 10021
(212) 570-9343

The Ralph Lauren Home
Collection
1185 Sixth Avenue
New York, NY 10036
(212) 642-8700

Ron Fisher Furniture
(800) 231-7370

Shaker Workshops
(800) 827-9900

Shayam Ahuja (fabrics and rugs)
201 East 56th Street,
New York, NY 10022
(212) 644-5910

Sleeping Partners
Tel: (212) 274-1211

Southern Pine Council
(504) 443-4464

Stephen-Douglas Antiques
Rockingham, VT 05101
(802) 463-4296

Sterling Plumbing Group, Inc.
(800) 783-7546

Steven J. Rowe Antiques
(603) 382-4618

Sunworthy Wallcoverings
(800) 535-7811

Sur La Table
(800) 243-0852

This End Up Home Collection
(furniture)
(800) 627-5161

Thomas Industries Inc.
(lighting)
(800) 825-5844

Thomasville Furniture
Industries
(800) 225-0265

Waverly Home
(wallpaper and fabrics)
(800) 423-5881

Margaret and Paul Weld,
American Antiques
(806) 635-3361

Westchester Marble & Granite
(800) 634-0866

# index